# Sex Over 40

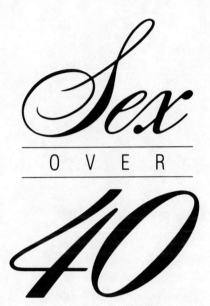

# Sex
### OVER
## 40

## SAUL H. ROSENTHAL, M.D.

**JEREMY P. TARCHER, INC.**
**Los Angeles**
Distributed by St. Martin's Press
New York

Library of Congress Cataloging in Publication Data

Rosenthal, Saul H.
  Sex over 40.

  Bibliography.
  Includes index.
    1. Sex instruction. 2. Middle age—Sexual behavior.
I. Title. II. Title: Sex over forty. [DNLM: 1. Sex—
in middle age—popular works. 2. Sex Behavior—in
middle age—popular works. HQ 31 R815s]
HQ31.R8433      1987      306.7'0880564      87-9903
ISBN 0-87477-432-2
ISBN 0-87477-495-0 (pbk.)

Jeremy P. Tarcher, Inc.
9110 Sunset Blvd.
Los Angeles, CA 90069

Distributed by St. Martin's Press, New York

Design by Tanya Maiboroda

Manufactured in the United States of America
10  9  8  7  6  5  4  3  2  1

First Edition

*This book is dedicated to
my wife, Cindy,
who has been my inspiration.*

# Contents

Acknowledgments    ix
Introduction: Why a Book About Sex Over 40?    xi

*PART I*
**HOW MEN AND WOMEN AGE SEXUALLY**    1

1. Sex and the Over 40 Male    3
2. Testosterone: The Hormone of Sexuality    15
3. How Women Over 40 Change Sexually    22
4. Estrogen Replacement After Menopause    31

*PART II*
**BECOMING A BETTER LOVER OVER 40**    43

5. Overcoming Erroneous Expectations
   about Male Sexuality    45
6. Overcoming Mental Obstacles to
   Really Good Sex    51
7. Sexual Variety: Romance and Sensual
   Adventures    61
8. Understanding Your Older Man    74
9. How to Help Your Man Get Firm Erections    80
10. A Guide for the Older Woman to
    Using Oral Sex    89
11. Enhancing Your Female Partner's
    Sexual Pleasure    99
12. More Ways to Please Your Woman Sexually    107
13. Prolonging Your Lovemaking for Hours    117

14. Simple Exercises to Strengthen Your
    Sexual Muscles    125
15. Masturbation for Older Men and Women    130

*PART III*
**SEX AND YOUR HEALTH OVER 40**    135

16. Satisfying Sex in Spite of Arthritis and
    Lower Back Pain    137
17. Painful Intercourse:
    It's Not "All in Your Head"    148
18. Sex in Spite of Heart Trouble:
    Continue to Enjoy It    154
19. Controlling Your Blood Pressure without
    Loss of Sexual Function    162
20. Prescription Medicines that Can Block
    Sexual Response    171
21. Drinking, Smoking, Drugs, and Sex Over 40    176
22. Prostate Problems, Sex, and the Older Man    188
23. Will a Hysterectomy Affect Your Sexual Life?    199

*PART IV*
**OVERCOMING ERECTION DIFFICULTIES**    209

24. Questions You Can Ask Yourself About Your
    Erection Problems    211
25. How We Evaluate and Treat Impotence    218
26. The Penile Implant: What It Is and
    How It Works    231

*CONCLUSION*
**SEX IN A LONG-TERM RELATIONSHIP**    243

Bibliography    255
Index    259
For More Information . . .    269

# Acknowledgments

I would first like to express my debt to the many patients who have provided the foundation of my knowledge about sexual function and dysfunction. Without them this book could not have been written.

While I was writing this book, many of my colleagues in other fields of medicine patiently answered my questions and read over drafts of chapters. I would especially like to thank Drs. William Fitch and Michael Newell in urology, Dr. Myron Zinn in cardiology, Dr. Sherwyn Schwartz in endocrinology, Drs. Joel Rutstein and Alfred Miller in rheumatology, and Drs. Mohammad Saidi and Richard Lackritz in OB/GYN.

My publisher, Jeremy Tarcher, had the vision to suggest this book and remained accessible to my questions and complaints throughout the publishing process. My editor, Ted Mason, had to put up with a stubborn and hardheaded author. I appreciate his patience and tact in working with me, as well as his many good suggestions. Kate Zentall, the copy editor for this book, made useful suggestions in substance as well as making the book easier to read. Lynette

Padwa, the production manager, put the book into its final form.

I want to give special thanks to my secretary, Kay McKey, who patiently typed interminable drafts of one chapter after another without complaint.

My brother Daniel started my writing in this area by suggesting my work on a newsletter dealing with sex and sexual dysfunction for men and women over forty.

Finally, and most importantly, I'd like to thank my wife, Cindy, who was my inspiration throughout. It was she who initially suggested that I write a book about sex over forty. She read the early versions of most of the chapters and made many useful suggestions. She also patiently put up with my spending long hours on nights and weekends writing the book and then going over draft after draft. I could not have accomplished what I did without her loving support.

# Introduction

# Why a Book About Sex Over Forty?

So often in my practice men and women over forty—good, solid, respectable men and women like yourselves—come to me at the point of desperation. They're afraid that their sexual lives are declining to extinction, and they don't really understand what's happening or what can be done. When they are in sexual situations these men and women feel humiliated, embarrassed, rejected, helpless, or just plain disappointed. It's easy to feel like a failure or to feel that you've lost your masculinity or femininity when sex isn't working.

It's tragic that this happens so frequently. These years should bring the most satisfying sexual experiences of a person's life and bolster feelings of self-esteem and success-fulness. In fact, many of the older men and women I see find that when their sexual lives are restored the *rest of their lives* becomes meaningful again.

It has always been difficult for men and women over forty to find sexual information intended *for them*—informa-tion that could help them understand the changes in their sexual lives. My discussions with older men and women have shown that there is a real need for a book about sex addressed directly to them.

At this point in your lives you have different sexual needs and sexual problems from people in their twenties and thirties. In spite of your special needs, however, there is very little written specifically for you—with specialized sexual information that deals directly with your sexual wants, your needs, and your problems.

A reliable source of practical information that will help you to understand and adjust to your changing sexual responses can be very important to you now. It can show you how to have a richer and more satisfying sexual life than you've ever had before by teaching you how to adapt to the natural changes that are occurring in your body.

Many of us were raised, and went through our sexually formative years, at a time when sexual information was not readily available. Undoubtedly our parents tried to teach us the various nonsexual skills that we needed to be healthy and successful people, but they often omitted teaching us anything about how to be good sexual partners. It's very possible that they didn't really know themselves.

In fact, it's more than likely that your parents sheltered you from whatever limited information may have been available at the time. Your upbringing may well have left you with many inhibitions about expressing your sexuality.

When you did learn about sex you couldn't imagine "older" men and women, the age of your parents and grandparents, ever engaging in it. Now that you're their age yourself, you're probably aware that sex is an important part of your life. You certainly don't want to lose the closeness, warmth, and intimacy that a good sexual relationship can bring.

As you get older you can't rely on sex just happening the way it did when you were younger. Men and women over forty undergo physical changes that, although normal and natural, affect their bodies' sexual responsiveness.

When you're over forty you can, and should, continue

to have good, even wonderful, sexual experiences—but having them requires knowledge, adaptation, understanding, innovation, and imagination. You have to be aware of what's going on in your body and your partner's body. You need to adapt to these changes with a willing and enthusiastic use of your imagination—and with a spirit of innovation.

Now your body no longer "does its thing" on its own without much help from you, the way it used to do when you were younger. You and your partner need to work together now, more than ever, to get the most out of your sexual lives. It's now much more important for you to make love spontaneously, to use variation freely, and to avoid letting sex become routine or dull. In this book I'll help you find ways to express your sexuality that are both imaginative and sensible.

In addition to experiencing the normal physical changes that I've already mentioned, men and women over forty unfortunately are more susceptible to a number of illnesses such as arthritis, high blood pressure, heart conditions, and diabetes that can affect their sexuality. If you have one of these conditions, you may also be required to take medications that can also cause sexual difficulties.

Considering that the sexual changes of aging are universal and that the sexual consequences of illness are common for men and women over forty, it is absolutely astounding that so little has been written to guide older men and women with their specific sexual needs. I will attempt to fill this gap by supplying you with the most recent information on the sexual side effects of various illnesses and medications as well as by suggesting the best ways to avoid these problems.

In order to adapt to your changing body's responses and to sexual problems caused by medical illnesses you may need to vary the lovemaking activities that you commonly use and the patterns of lovemaking that you're accustomed to.

Unfortunately, many people over forty have been

brainwashed with Victorian attitudes about sex. This closed-mindedness causes them to feel that they have few options available to them—that any sexual variation from whatever they have been doing for the last twenty-five years is probably immoral or perverse. Thus, their upbringing not only limits their knowledge of sexual options and variations, but it has left them with many inhibitions about what is right, proper, and appropriate.

Therefore, people over forty may often be less flexible about adapting to changes in their bodies and overcoming sexual difficulties. In this book, I will suggest many ways for you to accommodate your lovemaking to the situations you may face—ways that I hope almost anyone would feel comfortable with.

## WHY YOUR DOCTOR CAN'T ANSWER YOUR QUESTIONS ABOUT SEX

Your own physician may not have answers to your questions about how your body is functioning sexually. When I went to Medical School at Harvard in the late fifties and early sixties, we were never taught anything about sex —nothing about sexual function or the treatment of sexual problems. In fact, at that time there weren't any courses about sex at medical schools anywhere in the country. Yet when we physicians graduated from medical school, our patients came to us with sexual problems and expected us to be experts in the field.

Even now, although there has been a revolution in the scientific evaluation and treatment of sexual problems, these subjects have managed to win a very small place, if any, in most medical schools' curricula. Courses available to medical students are usually short courses or electives, if any are offered at all. It's therefore not surprising that so many doctors are uncomfortable talking about sexual problems. The truth is that they know little more about the subject than their patients.

Many an older man with an erection problem has been told with crushing finality, "At your age what do you expect!" One patient, whose sexual function I was able to restore with a simple adjustment of his blood pressure medicine, told me, "No one ever listened before. They all just said I needed an implant."

When you realize that most physicians were never taught about sexual problems in medical school, their lack of knowledge is really not surprising. They're busy working in their own fields, and they don't really have the time to acquire the specialized knowledge that's available on the treatment of sexual problems.

I became interested in treating patients with sexual dysfunctions around 1970 because I realized what a tremendous need there was for sexual therapy. At that time, only a relatively few years ago, treating sexual problems was a very daring thing to do. That in itself gives you an idea of how far we've come since then. In those years I was an associate professor of psychiatry at the University of Texas Medical School at San Antonio. I also introduced the teaching of basic courses in sexuality, sexual function, and sexual treatment to the medical students at the university.

I've continued to treat men and women with sexual dysfunctions for more than fifteen years and am currently in private practice and the director of the Sexual Therapy Clinic of San Antonio. Although I'm a psychiatrist and see psychiatric patients, the program I am involved with at the Sexual Therapy Clinic employs a comprehensive medical evaluation and treatment program that combines the skills of specialists in urology, endocrinology, gynecology, psychiatry, and other specialties.

Some years ago researchers didn't have the nerve to apply science and technology to sexual problems for fear of being labeled charlatans. In the past ten years, however, that situation has changed radically. From a scientific viewpoint, at least, the medical establishment's era of neglect of sexual dysfunction is over. Today's sexual treatment combines medicine and technology in a wide array of techniques ranging from hormonal and blood chemistry tests to the measurement of nighttime erections and the blood pressure of the penis. My colleagues and I at the Sexual Therapy Clinic do our best to use all of the latest scientific information when we diagnose and treat sexual problems.

Fifteen years ago the latest advance in treating sexual dysfunction was nonmedical sexual therapy based on the Masters and Johnson approach. This was a lot better than anything that had come before, but now sexual therapy without medical evaluation and treatment is simply no longer valid for people over forty.

I've tried to write a book that presents the important sexual information you need in clear, straightforward, helpful, and inoffensive language. You will receive the benefit of what I've learned at the Sexual Therapy Clinic—the most current and advanced information I've been able to obtain. There is no section on sexually transmitted diseases, as this subject is now touched on almost daily in the media. I felt that adequate coverage of it in this book would have taken space away from other material not so readily available to men and women over forty.

I hope that you will find many useful and helpful ideas in this book, and that it will help you to achieve a more open viewpoint about your sexuality. Different chapters will be meaningful to different people. Remember, however, that if you can find *one* important piece of information that will enrich your sexual life or help to restore your sexual functioning, it can revolutionize your entire life.

This book is filled with practical information for the individual, but the maximum benefit will come from sharing the book's ideas with your partner. Try to discuss the points that seem important to you. It may help both of you to read the most pertinent sections of the book together.

In the past, the two of you may have felt awkward about discussing sex and may never have developed a vocabulary of sexual words you felt comfortable with. I hope that the book will help to provide both a vocabulary and a framework for talking about the sexual issues in your lives.

I also hope that you and your partner will enjoy this book, and that it will add to the richness and fullness of your life experiences.

# PART I

# HOW MEN
# AND WOMEN
# AGE SEXUALLY

# 1

# Sex and the Over 40 Male

Jack R. came into my office reluctantly. He looked embarrassed and depressed. A well-dressed, conservative man in his early fifties, he obviously was used to success in meeting life's challenges. But at this point he wasn't feeling successful about his sexual life, and he seemed extremely discouraged about it.

He had decided that he was "becoming impotent." He doubted if he could be helped. He said he often was unable to get an erection. Moreover, the few times he did get hard, he would lose his erection before he climaxed.

It soon became clear that when Jack said that he wasn't getting erections anymore, he had a rather restricted definition of what that meant. What was actually happening was that he wasn't getting *spontaneous* erections anymore—that is, he wasn't getting erect without stimulation of his penis. (And, as it turned out, his wife was doing very little to provide the penile stimulation he needed in order to get erect.)

Jack's claim that he was losing his erections before climaxing was also misleading. Actually, he was maintaining his erections for quite a long time, but he was sometimes unable to climax, even with prolonged intercourse, and his erections would gradually fade.

This man was unaware that what he was experiencing is quite common and to be expected for a man of his age. Unfortunately, he was still expecting his body to respond the same way it did twenty years ago, so his body's natural responses at fifty put him into a tailspin.

I've treated this same unwarranted anxiety in many over-forty men, and I've observed that it's usually *lack of knowledge* concerning sexual response after forty that produces such heightened anxiety and distress.

Some of the changes in your body that I'm going to tell you about may seem somewhat scary at first. You may not like to hear them. But I'll also tell you how to deal with them successfully. Knowledge and a clear plan of how to respond to these changes are extremely important in maintaining an undiminished sex life as you get older.

When you're over forty, your penis may stop functioning the way you always expected it would. It may not get hard when you think it should, and it may act in other ways different from the ways you are used to. If you start thinking that this means sex is almost over for you, or that your penis will soon stop functioning totally, it can be very frightening.

Many of our feelings of self-worth, self-esteem, and masculinity are tied to how we feel about ourselves sexually. If a man feels that he's failing sexually, that "he can't get it up," it's hard for him to feel like a success in business or home life or any other area. There's always that nagging feeling in the back of his mind that he's really not successful anymore.

If you've started having difficulty getting erections effortlessly whenever you want them, if they're not coming as spontaneously as you'd like, if sometimes you don't seem to have the need or ability to ejaculate, you may start feeling the way Jack did—that your sexual ability is fading away and that it won't be long until it's gone. You've heard jokes and stories about sexually ineffective older men, and you may be frightened that you're losing your sexual powers also. This simply isn't true. Lovemaking doesn't have to diminish or end at forty, fifty, sixty—or at any age. On the contrary, think of this as a time to *change your approach to sex,* rather than give up on it, and you will learn to make your sexual life better than ever.

It's important to realize that the physical changes that occur throughout your body as you get older, while undeniable, don't require you to give up all the activities that you enjoy.

Some physical things *you may even do better* than when you were in your twenties. If you've taken up jogging in recent years, for instance, you may run a lot more now—and be able to run much farther—than you could when you were younger.

It's the same with sex. By learning to adapt to change, you may find it possible to be an even better lover than before.

## WHAT CAN YOU EXPECT?

Let's go over some of the natural bodily changes that occur as you get older. These changes are predictable and shouldn't surprise or upset you.

**You will need more direct stimulation in order to get erect.** One thing you can count on is that when you are over forty you won't be getting spontaneous erections in the same rapid and easy way you did when you were in your adolescence or early twenties. At that age, just the thought of sex, seeing your undressed partner, or a fantasy about a sexual situation would cause your penis to spring to attention in a matter of seconds. This just isn't going to happen anymore. As you mature, all the physiologic systems in your body slow down—including this one.

You will, without a doubt, take longer and longer to become erect from mental stimulation alone—just thinking about sex or seeing a sexual partner won't be enough. You will require more and more direct physical stimulation to your penis in order to get a good erection.

But that may not really be so bad. It certainly doesn't mean that you're going to stop having erections or stop having sex, only that your partner is going to have to help you get hard. And here, an understanding, loving partner is truly important. She can assist you by using her hands, her mouth, her breasts, or other parts of her body to stimulate your penis—and this can open a whole new chapter in your sex life, as your lovemaking becomes more mutual, sensual, and varied.

Too often at the Sexual Therapy Clinic of San Antonio I've seen couples who didn't realize that an over-forty man has a need for direct physical stimulation. In the past, his erections had come spontaneously. The woman had rarely touched the man's penis and he had never had any real need for it. Now, gradually, he was no longer getting spontaneous erections with any frequency. He kept waiting for them, though, before approaching his wife. Their sexual encounters became less and less frequent as he started waiting a week, two weeks, then a month at a time. Finally, the couple would come to see me, assuming that he was becoming impotent.

It's important to realize that you don't have to wait for an erection to start lovemaking. Your partner can help you get hard, and you can make love whenever the two of you desire.

**You may not be quite as firm.** A second important change for you to be aware of is that your erections will lose some of the "rock-hard" firmness they had when you were younger. They will still, however, be more than adequate and firm enough so that you can enter your partner with ease and you can both enjoy full satisfaction.

Firmness is, for the most part, a cosmetic issue: While your penis may not be as hard as it used to be, it can still do the job very well. It's not how hard your penis is but how well you use it (and the rest of your body) that will determine how much you please your partner during lovemaking.

***You'll need to climax less often.*** Many men over forty become concerned because they don't climax as readily or as easily as they used to, assuming this to be an early sign of impotence. One forty-eight-year-old patient of mine, Harold M., told me he was able to have intercourse, with a good erection, for almost thirty minutes at a time, but sometimes just wasn't able to get over the edge to climax. His complaint was that "the lovemaking really felt good, but it aggravated me that I couldn't come."

Unfortunately, instead of enjoying the experience, Harold allowed himself to get frustrated and annoyed. What he didn't realize was that as he had gotten older his body just didn't need to ejaculate as often as before. Nonetheless, he was still having intercourse just as often—so that now he was simply having intercourse more frequently than he needed to climax.

Masters and Johnson maintain that most men over sixty need only one or two climaxes per week. Some men cut down their frequency of lovemaking as they get older because of their decreased desire for ejaculation, but this isn't at all necessary. If you need a climax only once a week, you can still make love two or three times a week. You just have to be willing to adapt to the situation and to enjoy the many pleasures of lovemaking without pushing yourself to climax. If you pressure yourself to climax when your body doesn't really need to, you may strain and strain and eventually lose your erection and then feel that the experience was a failure instead of a success. This can change what should be a very enjoyable experience into a tense and anxious one. You'll end up worrying about whether you'll be able to climax the next time you make love, and if you have trouble climaxing again you may even begin to fear trying sex in the future.

Often my male patients feel that they're letting their partner down when they don't ejaculate. Sometimes a woman will feel that somehow she has failed sexually if her partner hasn't been able to reach a climax, that he no longer finds her attractive, or that he's been sleeping with somebody else.

Fifty-nine-year-old Henry B. came to my office desperate. He often was unable to climax during intercourse, and each time that happened it turned into a family catastrophe. His wife would cry and feel rejected and threatened. There was no way he could reassure her. He finally convinced her to come to the clinic with him for a consultation, and I explained to her that his occasional inability to ejaculate was due to his age rather than lack of love for her.

Remember that occasionally not climaxing is a natural occurrence after forty, one of the changes that you can easily adapt and adjust to. Lovemaking can be a very enjoyable sensual and sexual experience, with or without a climax. You don't need to climax every time you make love, and you shouldn't push yourself to. Just tell your partner in advance that you may not be able to climax so that she won't feel she's letting you down.

Making love without that pressure to ejaculate can add a new dimension to your relationship, making it more pleasurable for you and your partner to enjoy leisurely and prolonged intercourse.

*Lasting longer, enjoying more.* Now that your body is no longer pressuring you for quick ejaculations, you'll probably be able to enjoy intercourse longer than you could when you were younger. This can be a real plus for your partner. Women often require longer stimulation in order to become fully aroused and to climax. Your partner will thus enjoy your newfound sexual endurance, and you'll both enjoy being able to continue with longer, more sensual lovemaking.

*Waiting time between erections.* After climaxing, there is always a certain time period during which you are unable to get erect again. During this *refractory period,* your penis will be unable to respond, no matter what the stimulation.

When you were in your early twenties, you probably could get a second erection just a few minutes after climaxing. That few-minute rest period probably lengthened to twenty minutes when you were in your thirties and to an hour or two in your forties. By the time you're in your sixties, you may have to wait an entire day or more after ejaculation before you can get hard again.

The amount of time you'll need to wait varies somewhat with the amount of excitement that you're feeling. Under very stimulating circumstances your refractory period may be shortened, and you may be able to respond more quickly.

Awareness of the changes that come with maturing is again the key here. If you try to get hard again too soon after ejaculation, you will naturally have difficulty getting a good erection. If you and your partner aren't expecting this, you may both feel a sense of anxiety, failure, and disappointment.

When you try again several days later, even though you've had an adequate rest period, worry about your previous failure can cause you to have trouble getting hard again. In other words, you can scare yourself into an episode of temporary impotence.

A very sensible way for you and your partner to avoid this kind of unpleasant outcome is to accept your body's message. If you can't get hard because it's too soon after your last ejaculation, don't try to force it. You can enjoy a very sensual lovemaking experience without an erection by caressing each other manually or orally. You can certainly use manual or oral stimulation to satisfy your partner and help her climax. Then, when your body is ready again for intercourse, you'll be able to go at it with a fresh spirit and enthusiasm.

Remember, too, that if you don't ejaculate you usually won't need a long rest period. So if your erection fades without a climax, you should be able to get hard again fairly quickly.

*Other changes.* There are some other changes in the over-forty male that you may notice. When you ejaculate, for example, your semen will not be expelled with the same rocketlike force as when you were younger. The muscles behind the push aren't as strong as they used to be. This really shouldn't affect your enjoyment of your orgasms. After all, ejaculation isn't a distance contest.

When you were younger, you may have felt a sensation of impending ejaculation a few seconds before you actually climaxed. This is called "the feeling of ejaculatory inevitability." As you've gotten older, you have probably noticed that this feeling seems to blend in more with the beginning of your orgasm.

You may also observe that after you climax your erection recedes more quickly than it did when you were younger. This is also one of the inevitable changes of aging, but one that needn't affect your enjoyment.

## WHY THESE CHANGES OCCUR

Why these gradual changes as you pass forty? Why less need to ejaculate? Why more need for penile stimulation? Why slightly less hard erections?

The reasons are rather complicated. Erection, which you always experienced as a *simple* phenomenon—you saw your partner undressed, thought about sex, and your penis got hard—is actually a very *complex* process. It requires a precise interplay among various parts of your body. The first is your *brain,* as you respond to mental erotic stimulation and thoughts. The second is the erection reflex, which occurs when your penis is physically stimulated and impulses pass back and forth through your *nervous system.*

The nervous system acts by influencing a third mechanism, a series of synchronized *vascular* actions. Your arterial system has to provide an adequate blood supply to your penis, while at the same time a set of one-way valves in your penile veins acts to partially block the outflow of blood. This development pools the blood in special compartments in your penis and produces an effect like inflating a long, thin balloon. Your penis swells, becomes hard, and is ready for sex.

The whole system is primed by adequate amounts of the male hormone testosterone, which helps control your erection mechanism and is largely responsible for sexual desire and arousal.

That's the way erection works *ideally.* The trouble is that as you get older, this complicated system suffers some gradual wear and tear. Your reflex mechanism isn't as sharp. You may develop some degree of high blood pressure or hardening of the arteries in the vessels supplying blood to your penis. This results in a decrease in its blood supply and, consequently, the speed with which you can get hard.

The venous valve system also suffers wear and tear, and you may develop some microscopic leakage of the pooled blood back out of your penis. This prevents your erection from getting quite as hard as it once did.

Finally, with every decade, your body's level of testosterone decreases. You produce less at thirty than at twenty, less at sixty than at fifty. (I'll discuss testosterone more fully later.)

As the erection system loses some of its sharpness of response, you'll start to notice the gradual changes in your erection that we've already described—slower erections, more need for stimulation, less firmness. But while your erection mechanism may have become more fragile and requires more help, keep in mind that *it's still working effectively* and should continue to do its job, right up through your sixties, your seventies, and beyond.

For a minority of men, the erection system gets derailed, however, and a real impotence problem, with inability to get erect, develops. Why does this occur?

To begin with, some older men have more severe breakdowns in their erection mechanism than others. Some have illnesses, such as diabetes, that can cause damage to the nerves responsible for the erection reflex. Other men may suffer from pronounced hypertension, arteriosclerosis, or other conditions that may cause diminished blood supply to the penis.

Lack of testosterone may contribute to some men's problems. While the level of testosterone falls to some extent for every man, some men may develop a real deficiency.

Other extrinsic factors can unbalance an older man's more fragile erection mechanism—particularly alcohol, tobacco, and certain medicines, which we will describe at greater length in chapters of their own. Deficiencies of certain nutrients can play a part as well. Moreover, certain illnesses, pain, and—most important—anxiety and tension can all, individually or in combination, block your erection mechanism. These various factors that can potentially interfere with your erection prospects will be discussed more fully in subsequent chapters, along with ways you can maximize your chances for erection success.

## WHY LOVEMAKING CAN BE BETTER AFTER 40

Many women have told me they feel that older men make better lovers. When they explain why, it's clear that the sexual changes of maturity contribute a great deal to what women like about making love with older men.

Barbara M., forty-two, told me, "It sometimes takes me a little while to get sexually excited. My first husband, who was my own age, was immediately erect and impatient for me to get turned on. My current lover, who is ten years older, takes some time to get ready, the way I do. We both stimulate and arouse each other, and for me that's a big plus.

"Bob usually needs me to play with his penis before he can get hard. I like being *needed* to produce his erection. It's nice to be able to help, and it makes me feel proud and excited when I make him hard. I enjoy the feeling of his penis getting firmer and firmer as I play with it. I feel that he's getting hard in response to me instead of just starting off that way.

"Lovemaking also lasts a lot longer. Young men seem ready to ejaculate right from the beginning, but Bob actually needs my help to climax at times. I can usually bring him to climax by making strong, active movements during intercourse. It's really fun watching him as I move. It makes me feel as if *I'm* giving him his climax, and that makes me feel like a skilled and sexy lover. I also really feel appreciated.

"The whole experience is more tender and sensitive and sensual and lasts longer. I think that all women like this."

As a younger man, the dominant theme in your sex life was the need to ejaculate. You became erect with little or no direct physical stimulation and were always in a hurry to proceed to intercourse. While you may have felt proud of this ability then, the pressure for rapid intercourse and rapid ejaculation doesn't fit the needs of most women, who usually take a little longer to get sexually excited. They may find younger men impatient, self-centered, and not willing to take the extra time needed to help a woman get aroused as well.

Women desire and appreciate more direct physical stimulation prior to intercourse and are generally more appreciative of lovemaking as a prolonged, sensual experience of which ejaculation is only a part. As an older man, you'll find that you will also enjoy the fullness of the lovemaking experience when you please your partner as well as yourself.

You are better prepared for the role in many ways now that you are older. You've had more experience and more time to learn how to best please your partner. You also have less need to push ahead toward a quick ejaculation. The now more gradual, sensual lovemaking focuses less on your penis alone and more on the whole mental and physical experience. Older men are better equipped, both mentally and physically, to please their partners as well as themselves.

Making love with an older man may be a more *mutual* lovemaking experience in other ways as well. A younger man's erection is simply *there*, and a woman may feel that she has had very little to do with the producing of it. But in making love with an older man, that same woman will most likely have a much more active role. She'll have the pleasure and personal experience of bringing about that erection herself, with her own two hands. It can give her a feeling of power, participation, and mutuality in your sexual relations that she very well may not have had before.

Often I've had a woman say, as Barbara did, that she enjoys being *needed* in lovemaking. She feels proud when she can help her partner get hard and enjoys the feeling that he is becoming erect in direct response to *her,* and to what she is doing.

As an over-forty man coping with a variety of physical changes, you may feel that your need for penile stimulation represents a decline in your physical prowess. It is, however, simply a natural change, so don't overlook the great advantages in it for both of you.

You will, first of all, have the pleasure of your partner stimulating you in an endless variety of erotic ways. You'll also have the time and inclination to caress her at leisure, without being under internal pressure to hurry to ejaculate. And your partner will have the fun and enjoyment of exciting you, stimulating you, and helping you to get hard.

# 2

# Testosterone: The Hormone of Sexuality

Testosterone is the most active and powerful of the androgen hormones—the masculinizing, or male, hormones, produced by the testes and the adrenal glands. It regulates the development of male sexual features in young boys and teenagers, and it maintains male sexual features in later life. Testosterone also stimulates growth, the production of protein, muscular development, and the deposition of calcium in bones. In addition, as mentioned in the previous chapter, testosterone plays a very important role in regulating sexual performance and desire. In fact, testosterone seems to be the hormone most responsible for sexual drive, sexual interest, and sexual responsiveness—in women as well as men.

How, as a male hormone, can testosterone affect sexual desire in women? While androgens are considered to be male sexual hormones, they are actually produced in men and women alike and seem to control sexual desire in both.

Androgens are produced in the adrenal glands of both sexes in approximately equal amounts. They then travel in the bloodstream to the liver, where they're converted into testosterone.

The small amount of testosterone that women end up with seems adequate to produce sexual responsiveness for them. The male body, however, requires much more of this hormone. Men produce large additional amounts of it in their testicles, while women's ovaries are producing equally large amounts of the feminizing hormone estrogen. The extra testosterone that men produce in their testicles results in men having ten to twenty times more testosterone than women have.

Testosterone plays a major part in determining a man's levels of sexual desire, his ability to get an erection, and probably his ability to ejaculate as well. And it has a special significance to an older man, because the amount produced gradually decreases throughout his life, and this loss inevitably plays some role in the diminished sexual appetite and sexual response that may be experienced with aging.

Many factors go into sexual response besides testosterone, of course, including how much attraction you have to your partner, the sexual excitement of the situation, the absence of stress and anxiety, your erection reflex, the blood supply to your penis, and, finally, how directly your penis is stimulated. Unquestionably, though, a true deficiency of testosterone will interfere with the quality of your erections, even if all other circumstances are ideal.

## WHAT CAN TESTOSTERONE REPLACEMENT DO?

Can testosterone reverse problems of loss of sexual desire, erection ability, and ability to ejaculate? When it first became available, doctors used testosterone to treat any man who came along complaining of impotence. The results were generally disappointing, because in any group of impotent men only a minority have testosterone deficiency as the sole cause.

If you're experiencing these problems and your testosterone level is clearly deficient, testosterone replacement is worth a try. It can produce a striking and dramatic improvement. Unfortunately, however, even if your testosterone levels are deficient, hormone replacement isn't guaranteed to correct impotence, since erection difficulties have many possible causes. If nerve damage or blocked blood vessels, for example, are the cause of your problem, all the testosterone in the world won't facilitate erections.

## WHO SHOULD TRY TESTOSTERONE?

Many doctors feel that testosterone should be restricted to men who have clearly deficient levels. My own inclinations are somewhat different. If a man of sixty with erection problems has a "low normal" testosterone level, he may indeed still be within the "normal" range for a man in his sixties, but it's certainly much lower than the level he probably had when he was in his twenties. As his erection mechanism has become more fragile with age, he may now be on the border between getting erections or not getting them. The extra boost that restoring his testosterone level can give him may be all he needs to get him functioning again.

I have observed that many older men respond favorably to testosterone when their hormone levels are in the lower range of what is considered normal, especially when the hormone is prescribed in conjunction with other erection-improving medications. (See chapter 25 for more on this subject.)

## HOW IS TESTOSTERONE PRESCRIBED?

Clearly, testosterone has potential in restoring sexual vigor and desire for at least some older men. Let's review how it is administered.

Testosterone ordinarily has a brief life in the body,

since it is broken down rapidly in the liver. Additional testosterone taken orally isn't very effective, as it is quickly digested and destroyed. For this reason, longer-acting forms of testosterone have been developed, combining the hormone chemically in order to slow its breakdown in your body.

Methyltestosterone is one of the longer-acting forms that is not metabolized as rapidly as is plain testosterone. It can be taken in pill form or as a tablet that is absorbed under the tongue or through the cheek. The usual dosage is 10 mg to 50 mg per day in pill form or 25 mg under the tongue.

Most experts, however, feel that the oral administration of methyltestosterone is not as effective as injections of still longer-acting forms such as testosterone cypionate and testosterone enanthate. In men who are testosterone deficient, an injection of 300 mg to 400 mg of testosterone enanthate once a month will usually be quite effective. For some men, the dose won't last for a full month, so that 200 mg every two to three weeks will give better results, with more consistent hormone levels.

If the shots help but getting to a doctor every month is a problem, you can learn to administer them yourself. Or, since the shots are usually administered in the buttocks, it may be easier to have your partner give them to you.

After testosterone replacement begins, a hormone-deficient man will probably notice some improvement in his erection ability within two weeks. Some men don't really feel the full benefit of the treatment until the second injection, when the hormone level has been built up.

## POSSIBLE SIDE EFFECTS

You may be thinking that all this sounds much too easy and that there must be some problems associated with testosterone. You are right. Besides its benefit to sexual activity, testosterone has other actions, some of which can cause undesired side effects for a small number of people. The vast majority of men who take testosterone, however, will probably never experience any of the possible side effects listed below.

Testosterone may cause the kidneys to increase the amount of water and salt they retain. This rarely causes problems, though, except when the hormone is administered in extremely large doses, or if you already have kidney or liver trouble or congestive heart failure.

Salt and water retention can also cause trouble if you have high blood pressure, migraine headaches, or epilepsy. With the usual testosterone replacement therapy program, however, it is unlikely that enough salt and water will be retained to cause difficulty, even if you have one of these conditions.

Testosterone stimulates red blood cell production, so that large doses conceivably could cause excessive production of red blood cells, a rare condition known as *polycythemia*. In addition, testosterone increases blood levels of calcium, but not usually by amounts which are clinically significant.

Another property of testosterone is that it stimulates the sebaceous glands, which theoretically could cause acne. Nevertheless, I have yet to see acne produced in an older man by testosterone replacement.

Some testosterone is changed into estrogen during its breakdown. Therefore, if very large amounts are given, some breast enlargement due to the increased estrogen might possibly occur.

Testosterone also stimulates the cells of the prostate gland. For this reason, men taking it require regular checkups for signs of prostatic enlargement, and those men with cancer of the prostate must avoid it altogether, because it could stimulate the growth of that type of cancer cells. It is not believed, however, that testosterone will *cause* a prostate cancer if there isn't one there to begin with. While it is unlikely that you have cancer of the prostate, for safety's sake it's important to have your prostate checked before starting to receive testosterone and periodically while you are taking it.

In rare cases, testosterone causes excessive sexual stimulation and painful erections that won't recede, a condition known as *priapism.*

Very large doses of testosterone can send a false message to your pituitary gland that your testicles are putting out plenty of hormones. Your pituitary gland will therefore produce less of the hormones that ordinarily stimulate your testicles. This can result in a lowered sperm count, which may cause difficulty if a couple is trying to conceive. Large doses of testosterone may also cause some decrease in the size of your testicles, as they will have less work to do.

Diabetics receiving testosterone may have to adjust their dosage of insulin or oral hypoglycemic medicine, since testosterone may slightly alter their capacity to handle sugar.

In rare cases, oral methyltestosterone can cause a kind of jaundice. For this reason, people with liver disease should steer clear of the oral form. Available information isn't entirely definitive, but there are indications that the injectable form of testosterone avoids this problem. Some medical authorities, in fact, recommend using oral methyltestosterone for only six months, followed by a six-month rest period, because of the danger of liver problems and breast enlargement.

## AN ADDITIONAL POSSIBLE BENEFIT

New research indicates that lowered levels of testosterone are associated with increased risk of heart attack. A recent study published in 1987 in the *Journal of the American Geriatrics Society* indicates that these lowered testosterone levels are frequently found in older men who had once been heavy drinkers. The authors hypothesized that testosterone might protect the heart by increasing the proportion of high density lipoprotein cholesterol or by increasing the performance of heart muscle directly. (On the other hand, I should note that heavy drinkers also tend to be heavy smokers and the correlation of heart attacks with low testosterone levels could actually be related to heavy smoking on the part of these men.)

## IN SUMMARY

If you are over forty, your levels of testosterone have gradually decreased over the years. The slide began when you were about twenty years old. Some men in their fifties, sixties, and seventies still have adequate levels of testosterone, but others do not. These lower hormone levels may be associated with loss of desire, loss of potency, loss of ability to climax, and loss of ejaculatory ability.

If your hormone levels are deficient, the administration of long-acting testosterone may rapidly and strikingly restore sexual desire and erection ability. But it must be emphasized that there are many other causes for sexual dysfunction, and testosterone won't magically provide the answer to every problem.

Finally, testosterone can bring with it some possible serious side effects. How you might be affected will depend on your own unique medical condition and history. A thorough exam by and discussion with your own physician is therefore imperative before beginning any testosterone replacement.

# 3

# How Women Over 40 Change Sexually

Women in their fifties, sixties, and seventies have occasionally come to me with what you might think of as an unusual problem. These healthy, well-adjusted women were without sexual partners because they were divorced or widowed or because their husbands were chronically ill. What troubled each of them was that although she didn't have a sex partner, she continued to have strong sexual feelings that were difficult for her to deal with and control.

I remember Helen M. in particular, a woman in her mid seventies, widowed, very active, working in her own small business. A new sexual relationship with a man seemed unlikely, but she found herself having frequent sexual fantasies and often feeling sexually aroused. Helen was afraid that she might, in her words, "do something foolish," and was distraught because she felt that "nice older women" without sexual partners weren't supposed to feel sexual—and certainly weren't supposed to be as consumed with sexual fantasies and sexual feelings as she was.

Helen was reassured to learn that it was normal for her to continue to have sexual feelings. She eventually formed a satisfying sexual and emotional relationship with an old acquaintance, a man seven years her junior who greatly appreciated her positive outlook about lovemaking.

Many people believe in the same old nonsense that Helen did—that women lose their sexuality as they age, especially after menopause. A few women do, in fact, experience a loss of sexual desire after menopause, and other women may use menopause as an excuse to end sexual lives that have been, for them, emotionally or physically unsatisfying. Most women, however, don't report any loss of sexual interest, sexual arousal, or sexual enjoyment after menopause.

## SEX MAY BECOME MORE PLEASURABLE AFTER MENOPAUSE

If you enjoyed sex before menopause and if you continue to have the opportunity for regular sexual activity, there is no reason why lovemaking shouldn't continue to be at least as satisfying for you as it was in earlier years.

The years after menopause may coincide with the departure of your children. This gives you and your partner more privacy for lovemaking and less of the feeling of constant fatigue that comes with caring for small children.

In addition, you might have been worried during your childbearing years about becoming pregnant. Since menopause eliminates that possibility, it can mean increased sexual freedom for you.

Some women dislike having intercourse during their menstrual period or have discomfort with sex at this time. For these women, no longer having menstrual periods may be liberating and may mean expanded opportunities for comfortable, worry-free sexual relations.

After forty, women may also find that they're more relaxed about sex in general. During early years of sexual activity, many older women were still wrestling with their antisexual upbringings. They were often sexually inexperienced, hesitant to experiment, and unsure of how to please themselves or their partners.

For example, many women don't really learn how to climax until they've reached their thirties or forties. The discovery of orgasm is just the beginning of learning a wide range of techniques for enhancing lovemaking. As women become better at lovemaking and start enjoying it more, they tend to become much more uninhibited and interested in learning more about their sexuality. For these reasons, women over forty who are happy with their sexual partners often tend to find their sexual lives more satisfying than when they were younger.

As a woman over forty, you will likely be more sexually assured and secure and have more knowledge of your own physical responses. You've continued to improve your sexual skills, you've gradually shed sexual inhibitions over the years, and you've learned to identify your sexual needs and preferences. You may feel more secure about trying new techniques, such as oral stimulation, or new positions for intercourse. While at earlier times in your life you may have been reluctant to tell your partner what you like sexually, you are probably now more open and able to communicate. Nonetheless, you shouldn't ignore the fact that, as a woman over forty, you are undergoing certain physiological changes that may affect your sexuality.

## YOUR HORMONE LEVEL
## FALLS ABRUPTLY AT MENOPAUSE

In previous chapters, we discussed how a man's body gradually undergoes physical changes and how these changes can affect his sexual response and desire. We also described how the hormone testosterone, which is the primary hormone responsible for sexual function in men, diminishes over the years. This slow decrease, as well as other imperceptible changes due to age, cause a man's sexual changes to be gradual, rather than sudden.

A woman, on the other hand, in addition to the slow changes of aging, experiences a sudden, possibly jolting decrease in her female sexual hormone, estrogen, at the time of menopause. Unless that estrogen is replaced, she may have more abrupt physical changes in her sexual organs than a man has. On the other hand, because estrogen is not responsible for sexual desire, she usually won't experience the slowing of sexual response and desire that men do.

## SEXUAL RESPONSIVENESS AND SATISFACTION REMAIN CONSTANT

Testosterone, which in women is produced in the adrenal glands and ovaries, is responsible for sexual desire in both women and men. The few women who do experience a loss of sexual desire at the time of menopause can probably attribute it to a decrease in their supply of testosterone, rather than to a loss of estrogen. Lack of estrogen seems to cause diminished desire only when physical changes brought on by its absence cause sex to become uncomfortable.

Since a woman's physical sexual responsiveness is usually maintained after menopause, you should experience little change in your ability to become aroused or to achieve orgasm after menopause. Helen, whom we described at the beginning of this chapter, may have been somewhat unusual in the intensity of her sexual desire, but many women in their fifties, sixties, and seventies report that their sexual desire continues just as strong as it ever was. Older women often report sexual dreams, as well as multiple orgasms during lovemaking. Moreover, many older women, even those at an advanced age, continue to masturbate if they are without a sexual partner.

The average age of menopause, which is occurring later

and later for women in America, is now about fifty. This is
five years later than it was for your mother's generation, and
ten years later than for your grandmother's.

## ESTROGEN WITHDRAWAL
## AT MENOPAUSE

We all know that some women go through periods of extreme discomfort at the time of menopause. Symptoms can
manifest themselves both emotionally (in anxiety, irritability, insomnia, nervousness, or depression) and physically
(with hot flashes, fatigue, and headaches). All of these are
indications of *acute estrogen withdrawal,* of the body complaining about a precipitous drop in hormone levels. These symptoms can last anywhere from six months to as long as five
years.

Not all menopausal women experience high levels of
discomfort. Those with less sudden or less severe declines in
their estrogen levels may notice few symptoms if any. In
fact, only about 15 percent of menopausal women report
major distress from hot flashes and other manifestations of
acute withdrawal.

There is no reason for any woman to have to undergo
prolonged discomfort from estrogen withdrawal. These
days, symptoms can be rapidly relieved by estrogen replacement therapy, which is usually readily prescribed for most
women with acute menopausal distress.

## LONG-TERM SEXUAL EFFECTS OF
## CHRONIC ESTROGEN DEPRIVATION

Hot flashes and the other signs of acute withdrawal are only
the tip of the iceberg. Because menopause represents a permanent decrease in the amount of estrogen your body is
producing, and because your body has stopped producing a

large proportion of this important hormone, certain long-term effects will become evident within five to ten years after menopause.

The potential changes from chronic estrogen deprivation can be simply stated. Estrogen is specifically involved with the maintenance and development of your sexual organs, so a sudden diminution in the supply of estrogen causes those organs to essentially atrophy, or shrink.

Thus, if you suffer a marked decrease in your estrogen level at menopause and you don't have estrogen replacement, you'll notice a gradual thinning of the walls of your vagina. When your ovaries were producing adequate estrogen, your vaginal walls were made up of thick, cushiony folds that allowed for a great deal of elasticity and expansion. It's this elasticity and ability to expand that allowed your vagina to accommodate a penis during intercourse and the passage of a baby during childbirth.

But the loss of estrogen following menopause causes a condition known as atrophic vaginitis. Your vaginal walls thin and become smooth, losing their soft folds and the cushioning effect they previously had. The loss of elasticity may also cause narrowing of your vagina's opening, shortening of its length, and narrowing of its width.

Losing estrogen will also result in a loss of vaginal lubrication. Both the speed at which you lubricate and the amount of lubrication may decrease. When you were younger, your lubrication may have begun after just ten to thirty seconds of sexual stimulation. Now, it may take a couple of minutes, and you may not get quite as wet.

The combination of these symptoms of chronic estrogen deprivation—loss of vaginal elasticity and cushioning, narrowing of the vaginal opening, and the decrease in lubrication—can combine to make sexual intercourse uncomfortable. You may experience pain either on initial penetration or with deep thrusting by your partner.

Occasionally, older women also report urinary symptoms, such as burning, after intercourse. This is due to direct irritation of the urinary passage and bladder, since they are no longer as well cushioned or protected by the vaginal lining during intercourse.

A few women with severe estrogen depletion may experience painful uterine contractions during orgasm. These spasms can be eliminated with estrogen replacement.

Without estrogen replacement after menopause, most women are likely to have some of the physical effects of decreased estrogen described above. Even so, their sexual interests and desires usually remain constant, and most women continue to enjoy a full sexual life.

On the other hand, a minority of women do report some loss of sexual desire following menopause. In some cases, the loss of desire is because sexual relations are uncomfortable due to lack of lubrication, narrowing of the vaginal opening, or other physical conditions. Other women may never really have enjoyed lovemaking (for more complex psychological or relationship-affiliated reasons), and they use menopause as a convenient reason to discontinue it. Still others may become self-conscious about their appearance and self-image, or may find their partner unattractive. Finally, for some women, as we mentioned above, diminished desire can result from lack of testosterone accompanying the loss of estrogens.

## SOME PHYSICAL ASPECTS OF SEXUALITY UNLIKELY TO CHANGE

Although your breasts may lose some elasticity and may not swell as much during sexual arousal as they did when you were younger, your nipples will continue to become hard, erect, and sensitive with stimulation. If you enjoyed having your breasts caressed in the past, you should continue to do so after menopause.

Your clitoris will continue to respond to stimulation in much the same way it did prior to menopause. It will still

become erect and firm, although because it may take somewhat longer to respond, you may desire more direct stimulation than you did earlier in your life.

Most women notice little if any change in their orgasms. Although laboratory measurements of uterine contractions during orgasm indicate that they may be somewhat
less powerful and of shorter duration after menopause, most
women report that they can't perceive any change in their
own climaxes.

## NONSEXUAL BODILY CHANGES
## DUE TO CHRONIC LACK OF ESTROGEN

Chronic estrogen depletion can bring on bodily changes that
are not necessarily sexually oriented. Following menopause,
many older women suffer from a marked acceleration of the
loss of their bone calcium, for instance, due to estrogen loss
as well as other factors. This may result in bones throughout
the body becoming thin and fragile, resulting in a dangerous
condition known as *osteoporosis.*

Severe osteoporosis can cause easy fractures of the hip,
arm, or spinal vertebrae. This process of accelerated bone
loss may be extremely prominent in women who have had
an early menopause or have had their ovaries surgically
removed earlier in life.

Osteoporosis isn't a minor or rare problem. We all
know of older women who have fractured their hips and
then been permanently incapacitated. Osteoporosis seems to
be especially prevalent among women who are white and
thinly built, who are heavy smokers, or who have a family
history of osteoporosis. As many as 25 percent of white
women over sixty may have spinal compression fractures
due to osteoporosis.

Arteriosclerosis and heart disease may also be accelerated by the absence of estrogen. Women who are
premenopausal seem to experience much less heart disease

than do men of the same age. But after menopause, when
women are no longer apparently "protected" by estrogens,
their rates of arteriosclerosis and heart attacks tend to equal-
ize up to men's.

Some women suffer a great deal of estrogen loss at
menopause, while others experience much less. Therefore,
while all postmenopausal women do experience some physical effects of estrogen withdrawal, the degree varies widely.
Probably about 25 percent of women suffer severely from
chronic estrogen deprivation if they don't have their estrogens replaced.

We'll be talking more about the role of estrogen in the
next chapter.

# 4

# Estrogen Replacement After Menopause

With so many uncomfortable and possibly serious problems that can be caused by lack of estrogen, you may wonder why estrogen replacement therapy isn't universal for all postmenopausal women. One reason, as I suggested earlier, is that women with serious symptoms are in the minority. But a more important explanation is that estrogen is an active hormone and may have unwelcome side effects of its own.

Before the 1940s and 1950s, menopause was conceived of as a natural and irreversible event. Symptoms of estrogen deficiency were simply considered inconveniences that older women had to endure. The most immediate discomforts of estrogen withdrawal, such as hot flashes, were treated with sedatives and exercise.

When estrogens became readily available three or four decades ago, doctors quickly realized that estrogen replacement therapy (ERT) would arrest the immediate symptoms of estrogen withdrawal such as hot flashes, but it soon became evident that ERT could also prevent other, long-term effects on the vagina and skeletal bones. It's no wonder, then, that ERT rapidly became the standard therapy. By the 1960s, many claimed that women could stay young forever by taking estrogens.

## THE UTERINE CANCER SCARE

Then, in the mid 1970s, the pendulum swung the other way. Reports of increased cancer of the uterus (endometrial cancer) among women taking ERT frightened many into stopping their estrogen therapy. This occurred despite the fact that uterine cancer is a very uncommon form of cancer, so that even with the indicated increase there was a very low incidence, and despite the additional fact that many more older women die each year from fractured hips due to osteoporosis—partly from estrogen deficiency—than ever die from uterine cancer. Some women who had had hysterectomies even forgot that with no uterus they were in no danger from uterine cancer. Doctors became very apprehensive about estrogen replacement therapy, and large numbers of women who might have been candidates for ERT were not treated with it. By the late 1970s, estrogen replacement therapy was generally used only if absolutely necessary, in the smallest dose and for the shortest time possible.

The medical community first hoped that estrogen creams could fill the gap and treat vaginal symptoms without exposing patients to the dangers of uterine cancer. These creams were applied topically to prevent vaginal shrinkage and dryness, but it soon became clear that the estrogen in the creams was rapidly absorbed. This resulted in the same blood levels of estrogen and caused similar risks as taking the hormone in pill form.

## ESTROGEN/PROGESTERONE CYCLING

After much investigation into ERT, a number of researchers reasoned that perhaps the trouble was caused by administering estrogen steadily and without a break—and in giving it alone without *progesterone,* the other ovarian hormone that accompanies estrogen during the last two weeks of each menstrual cycle.

To explain why this should be so we need a brief review of menstruation. In a normal menstrual cycle, estrogen stimulates the lining of the uterus (the endometrium) during the days before ovulation. Progesterone begins to be produced in significant amounts at the time of ovulation and accompanies estrogen until several days before menstruation. The combination of the two hormones the latter part of the cycle produces an orderly buildup of cells to prepare the uterine lining for the possibility of pregnancy. At the end of the month, if no fertilized egg is implanted, the amounts of both hormones decrease sharply. The uterus then sheds its old, unused lining in the menstrual period and gets ready to start anew.

When menopausal women having ERT would receive daily doses of estrogen, without a break and without accompanying progesterone, it caused the lining of the uterus to be constantly stimulated and to grow in a disorderly fashion. Researchers believed it was this persistent stimulation and uneven cell growth that led to increased danger of uterine cancer.

Some doctors then began to recommend that their patients take estrogen only five days per week or else three weeks out of the month, in order to interrupt the constant stimulation. But the women's body fat stored the estrogen and released it during the days they weren't taking the hormone, so the uterus was still, in fact, receiving continuous estrogen stimulation. Progesterone was what was needed to promote orderly growth, as well as necessary shedding.

Current evidence reveals that the uterine lining of postmenopausal women being cycled with a combination of estrogen and progesterone doesn't have the piling up of cells that comes from continuous estrogen stimulation; instead, it is normal in appearance.

In the early 1980s, a number of studies indicated that while postmenopausal women receiving estrogen alone had a higher rate of uterine cancer than did untreated postmenopausal women, those who received estrogen in combination with progesterone did not. In fact, women who took estrogen and progesterone cycled monthly actually turned out to have fewer cases of uterine cancer than did the untreated population.

This finding means that estrogen replacement therapy with progesterone may even protect women from getting uterine cancer—in addition to helping prevent osteoporosis (bone thinning), hip fractures, vaginal atrophy, and loss of vaginal lubrication.

## ERT AND BREAST CANCER

Even though cycled estrogen and progesterone seems to eliminate the danger of cancer of the uterus, concern has remained that estrogen might increase risk of breast cancer. Occasional reports in the past have suggested some link. More recently, however, larger and more comprehensive studies have indicated that there is no association between estrogen replacement and breast cancer.

I know of no study involving the long-term effects of estrogen and progesterone cycling on the incidence of breast cancer in postmenopausal women, although some investigators speculate that cycling may protect women against breast cancer as well as uterine cancer.

The predominant medical opinion at present, then, seems to be that estrogen replacement therapy does not increase your risk of getting breast cancer.

# ERT AND CARDIOVASCULAR DISEASE

One of the many potential benefits of adequate estrogen levels is that the danger of heart attacks and arteriosclerosis may be reduced. Indeed, studies seem to show that postmenopausal women taking estrogen have a lower average annual death rate from all causes, but especially from cardiovascular disease, than do postmenopausal women who are not taking estrogen. The implication is that *not* taking estrogen increases the risk of cardiovascular disease. Remember that while the risk of death from uterine cancer is relatively small, the risk from cardiovascular disease is relatively large, so that avoiding estrogen therapy could entail a significant danger.

On the other hand, nothing about estrogen is noncontroversial. Recent major studies have come up with conflicting results. Some even have seemed to show that women taking estrogen have higher rates of cardiovascular disease rather than lower, but as far as I can tell, the prevailing medical opinion seems to be that estrogen offers significant protection when it comes to heart and vascular disease.

# ERT CAN DECREASE OSTEOPOROSIS

As evidence accumulates, it is clearer and clearer that a major factor in the onset of osteoporosis in postmenopausal women is lack of estrogen, rather than simple aging. In 1984, the National Institute of Health called estrogen replacement therapy the most effective single therapeutic agent in preventing osteoporosis in postmenopausal women. The panel pointed out that osteoporosis causes more than 1 million fractures a year in women forty-five and older. They recommended the use of estrogen for most women who have had their ovaries removed before age fifty and suggested that all women undergoing natural menopause should be considered for estrogen therapy as well.


## CURRENT MEDICAL OPINION ABOUT ERT

It appears that estrogen replacement therapy, when combined with progesterone, is rapidly returning as standard treatment for postmenopausal women. As an article in *Medical Tribune* put it, "In every risk-benefit ratio, the scale is tipping toward the benefits of estrogen."

As mentioned before, however, some physicians still maintain that the dangers of estrogen replacement outweigh the risks, while others feel very conservatively that one shouldn't interfere with nature: if a woman's estrogen runs out when she's fifty-five, then so be it—the symptoms of estrogen deprivation are just a natural consequence of aging. Still other doctors, fearful of malpractice suits, hesitate to prescribe anything they may be criticized for in the future, even if the evidence now strongly favors it.

It's important to remember that, as with so many aspects of medicine, prevailing attitudes can change with new research and new studies. The pendulum may again swing away from ERT sometime in the future.

Right now, however, it appears that estrogen and progesterone cycling can protect a woman from the sexual effects of chronic estrogen deprivation. In addition, the best evidence seems to be that this treatment causes no increased danger of cancer of the uterus and probably is even protective. It also seems to be a major factor in protecting against osteoporosis and probably is protective against cardiovascular disease as well.

## ADMINISTERING ESTROGEN/PROGESTERONE CYCLING

Estrogen replacement therapy is usually prescribed in the form of a combination of several kinds of estrogen (called "conjugated estrogen," which includes Premarin and other brands). The estrogen is given for the first twenty-five days of each month, followed by five days without it, in a usual dose of 0.625 mg of conjugated estrogen, although a larger dose may be needed for some women. A smaller dose may offer some protection to the vagina in certain cases, but it is apparently insufficient to protect against osteoporosis.

Progesterone is added from day sixteen through day twenty-five. It's usually given in the form of medroxyprogesterone (Provera and other brands), at 10 mg per day.

## SOME WOMEN SHOULDN'T HAVE ERT

As we have mentioned before, estrogen is not for everyone. Because it can exacerbate certain medical conditions, some women will have to avoid it altogether, while others will need to be closely monitored by their doctors. Check carefully with your personal physician to find out whether estrogen/progesterone cycling is safe for you.

Any of the following conditions usually preclude a woman from ERT therapy:

- myocardial infarction (heart attack)
- thrombophlebitis (blood clots)
- undiagnosed vaginal bleeding
- cancer of the breast
- pulmonary emboli
- liver disease

A doctor will also be particularly vigilant if a woman in ERT therapy has migraine headaches, gall bladder disease, multiple sclerosis, high blood pressure, or seizure disorders (epilepsy) all of which can be worsened by estrogens. Caution must be exercised as well if a woman has endometriosis or fibrocystic disease of the breast, or if there is a family history of high blood fat levels (hyperlipidemia). One's doctor is the person to evaluate these factors.

Any woman starting estrogen replacement therapy should have a thorough physical, including a breast and pelvic exam, a Pap smear, a blood pressure check and possibly a chemistry profile. A mammography and an endometrial (uterine) biopsy prior to treatment are also advised by some, though most other doctors find these to be impractical and unnecessary.

After receiving the green light from your physician and beginning estrogen replacement therapy, you may experience some bleeding each month, similar to a light menstrual period, during those days when you are not taking the hormones. This indicates a natural shedding of the uterine tissue, just as it was shed before your menopause. But be observant: if bleeding occurs when it shouldn't, during the days that you *are* taking estrogen, this may signal some uterine pathology, and you'll likely need an endometrial biopsy (a simple office procedure). See your physician immediately should this occur.

Some medical authorities suggest an annual endometrial biopsy as appropriate follow-up for all women on ERT, while others maintain that one every two years is sufficient. Still others feel that routine biopsies are wholly unnecessary unless there are clinical indications for them.


## IS ERT FOR YOU?

Let's start with possible objections first. One of your considerations in deciding whether to engage in estrogen replacement therapy is whether you're willing to tolerate periodic bleeding similar to light menstrual periods. Even though this may involve only a day or two of light flow each month, some women will object to it and wonder why they should resume having any period at all when they could be rid of them forever.

As we have indicated, the potential benefits of ERT are considerable. Relief can be found for such estrogen withdrawal symptoms as irritability, insomnia, and hot flashes. Moreover, an active, enjoyable, and comfortable sex life can become physically easier. To quote one authority, Dr. P. W. Budoff, "Women who hope to continue an active sexual life into their late fifties, sixties, and seventies may want to consider ERT. Estrogen will not make you young again, but it can have a profound effect on your vagina, which returns to its youthful state very quickly after estrogen replacement therapy has begun and will maintain itself as long as replacement continues." While discomfort during intercourse due to lack of estrogen can have damaging effects on your intimate and loving relationship with your partner, comfort and relaxation during sex can immeasurably improve mutual satisfaction as well as your self-esteem. Finally, estrogen has a profound effect on maintaining your bone strength and preventing osteoporosis with its risk of fractures. It may also decrease your risk of heart disease and your risk of arteriosclerosis.

## CAN I GET PREGNANT IF I USE ERT?

You may wonder whether pregnancy is possible when monthly bleeding resumes. The answer: If you're past menopause, you cannot get pregnant. Although the estrogen/progesterone cycling can produce normal uterine lining and monthly shedding, it cannot produce new eggs from your ovary.

## OTHER OPTIONS BESIDES ERT
## FOR MAINTAINING SEXUAL ENJOYMENT

Many alternatives are available to help keep your lovemaking enjoyable and your vagina healthy, whether or not you choose to take estrogen replacement therapy.

To begin with, maintain an active sexual life if possible. Masters and Johnson have reported that women in their sixties and seventies who continue to have sexual contact once or twice a week continue to lubricate quickly and well. These women also continue to have good vaginal expansion during intercourse in spite of their age, their lack of estrogen, and the thinning of their vaginal walls.

There may be a time in your life when your partner is not available or when you don't have a partner. If so, one way to keep physically toned and sexually responsive until you do have a partner again is by masturbating. Postmenopausal women who are unable to have sexual relations but don't remain physically active through masturbation may experience some narrowing of the vaginal opening and shortening of the vaginal canal. As a result, they may have some temporary discomfort when they resume sexual relations in the future.

Some women occasionally insert a penis-sized object in their vagina during masturbation. Appropriately shaped dildos or vibrators are available in sex shops in some big cities, through mail order catalogues, and through some sexually oriented magazines.

One of my patients, Harriet M., shyly told me that she was embarrassed to buy a vibrator, so she simply used a cucumber or squash. She said they were just the right shape, were inexpensive and readily available, and had no sharp edges. She smilingly said that the only problem she had was blushing at the grocery store checkout counter.

Of course, anything you insert in your vagina should be clean, and long enough so that you can extract it easily.

Another way to keep yourself in shape is to tone your pelvic muscles by doing Kegel exercises, which are recommended after childbirth to reestablish vaginal tone—but which you can also use to keep your own vaginal tone healthy. These exercises are easy and can be done almost anywhere. They'll be described at greater length in chapter 14.

*Vaginal lubricants.* If you find that your vaginal lubrication is diminished, these can greatly help to prevent painful intercourse, as well as irritation of the urinary passages following intercourse. There is a great variety of choices.

Petroleum jelly (in the form of Vaseline) is fairly widely used. We don't recommend it, however, since it's not water soluble and can clog your pores and urinary passage. Surgical jellies do the job adequately and are easily washed off, but they certainly aren't aesthetic and may detract from your sexual mood. We prefer such vegetable oils as corn oil or safflower oil, which are smooth and provide good lubrication. Because they're edible they don't detract from oral sex. (They're also high in polyunsaturated fats and have no cholesterol.) One disadvantage: they can stain bedsheets.

Other vaginal lubricants are made especially for lovemaking. One we enjoy is Kama Sutra Oil Of Love, which is scented, tastes good, and imparts a warming feeling when you rub it or blow on it. It's available in specialty shops and some boutiques. Albolene Cream has also been recommended to us on several occasions. This clear, odorless, creamlike skin cleanser doesn't dry up and lose its lubrication and seems to work very well as a sexual lubricant.

The product Lubrin is specifically designed to be a vaginal lubricant and to be used during sex. It comes in vaginal inserts that dissolve internally within five minutes. Unscented and colorless, it washes off easily, and the manufacturers claim that it won't stain fabrics the way vegetable oils may do. It won't provide the sensuality a flavored lovemaking oil like Kama Sutra will, but as a simple vaginal lubricant it ought to be quite effective.

Finally, one highly inventive patient told me that she

uses the juice of an aloe vera leaf as a vaginal lubricant, and
that she and her partner are very happy with it.

## OTHER OPTIONS BESIDES ERT
## TO HELP PREVENT OSTEOPOROSIS

If you are unable to take estrogen because of medical problems, there are other ways in which you can help prevent
osteoporosis. Adequate lifelong calcium intake is very important. Calcium supplementation during the postmenopausal years can also help you slow down or avoid loss.

The addition of vitamin D and fluoride to a postmenopausal woman's diet has been shown to be effective in
retarding the progression of osteoporosis once it has been
diagnosed. These should be taken, however, only under the
direct supervision of a physician to avoid overdosage. (Excessive vitamin D, for instance, can cause kidney stones.)

One of the most important things you can do to maintain your bone structure and prevent osteoporosis is to get
adequate amounts of moderate exercise. Inactivity contributes greatly to loss of bone substance. Again, the best advice
on this and any questions regarding your unique condition
will come from your own personal physician.

# PART II

# BECOMING A BETTER LOVER OVER 40

# 5

# Overcoming Erroneous Expectations about Male Sexuality

One of the paradoxes of an older man's life is that he can order nearly every part of his body to do his will—but his penis, whose behavior is so important for his self-esteem, seems out of his control and often behaves in ways that are very frustrating for him. In fact, the more he anxiously tries to control it, the more trouble he's likely to have.

He can't get his penis erect by sheer will. He has to wait for the appropriate stimulation to make it happen. The more he worries or tries to get hard, the less likely he is to succeed. He feels embarrassed and humiliated if he doesn't get erect when he thinks he should, and he fears being a failure in his partner's eyes.

Men over forty, therefore, often have great concern about their sexual lives and a great deal of anxiety about their sexual performance. They often believe they have to live up to unrealistic expectations about male sexual performance—expectations that a real man can have an erection whenever he wishes, unassisted and without help, that his erections are always full and firm, that he constantly feels ready for sex, and that he can always make love to his partner anytime she desires.

These expectations are difficult to live up to at *any* age, but after forty, most men can't even come close to such unrealistic goals.

In my practice treating impotence and other sexual dysfunctions, I see a great many older men, and I'm constantly struck by how many of them are plagued by these same unrealistic expectations and by how these expectations contribute to their sexual problems.

I remember George M., sixty-five, who told me that his wife wouldn't touch his penis because she was "an old-fashioned woman." His goal was to get unassisted erections from caressing her "the way I always did." I had to tell him that those days were gone forever, but that if his wife realized that *he needed her help,* she probably would be glad to assist (she was), and that they would then both enjoy love-making more than ever (which they did).

Sometimes unrealistic expectations create sexual problems when there are none. Men begin to worry so much about not living up to those expectations that that in itself causes genuine sexual dysfunctions. A man with enough anxiety about his performance may end up actually unable to get erect, unable to maintain his erection, or ejaculating too rapidly because he is hurrying to use his erection before he loses it.

Patients frequently come to me with one or more of the following five complaints, which often turn out to have their origin in erroneous expectations.

## "I'M NOT GETTING ERECTIONS ANYMORE"

Too many older men tell me they're not getting erections anymore and have even stopped having sexual relations, when there is really nothing wrong with them at all! What they mean when they say they're not getting erect is that they are no longer experiencing the frequent, *unassisted* erections they got years ago.

Now that you're over forty, sooner or later you're going to require more direct physical stimulation of your penis in order to get hard. This doesn't happen to all men at the same age, but as you get older you'll certainly find that spontaneous erections happen less and less frequently. If you and your wife keep waiting for that spontaneous erection to occur before starting sex, you may eventually find yourself waiting a month or more.

Having your partner help you get hard is natural and normal—and besides, it can be fun for both of you. *Your erections may not be spontaneous anymore, but your lovemaking can be as spontaneous as you like.* You can make love whenever the mood strikes the two of you, as long as your partner is willing to help.

## "MY ERECTIONS AREN'T ROCK-HARD THE WAY THEY USED TO BE"

That's right, they probably aren't. Your erections at age forty, fifty, sixty, or seventy will probably not be as hard as they were when you were eighteen. So what! As long as they're hard enough for enjoyable lovemaking, they can give you and your partner all the pleasure you want.

You're probably a much more skilled lovemaker now than you were at twenty, and you are probably much more effective at pleasing a woman now than you ever were then, even though your erections may have been harder in those days.

Many men have the erroneous belief that their proficiency as lovers is in direct proportion to the hardness of their erections. Worrying about how hard your erection is will only serve to interfere with your excitement—and that will just make the erection softer. So stop measuring the hardness of your erection and just go ahead and enjoy it.

## "I CAN'T HOLD MY ERECTIONS"

Many men I treat believe that they're entitled to only one erection per sexual encounter. They feel that one erection has to last the entire lovemaking time—whether it be five minutes or forty-five minutes—and that once it's lost it's gone for good.

There's no reason this should be so at all. Where is it written that you're allowed to have only one erection? During the course of extended foreplay your erection may come and go three or four different times, even if you stay mentally very sexually excited and desirous. There's nothing wrong if this happens. It's perfectly natural. So if you have an erection and lose it, either prior to entry or even during intercourse, there's no reason for panic and no reason to feel ashamed. Just ask your partner to help you get your erection back, or stimulate her orally or manually until your erection returns. She'll appreciate the extra lovemaking as much as you do.

If you're getting firm erections, losing them during lovemaking becomes a problem only if it happens whenever you attempt to penetrate, preventing you from enjoying intercourse at all. This probably means that the problem is being caused by anxiety about your performance.

## "SOMETIMES WHEN WE HAVE SEX I CAN'T EJACULATE"

It's surprising how many men worry that they have a serious sexual problem because they occasionally can't reach a climax. When this has happened, what they've often done has been to attempt to *force* the climax, working harder and harder at it, until they become frustrated, scared, and lose their erections.

Most older men discover that even though they may be fully aroused and excited, they don't have the need to climax every time they have sex. They learn to accept this as a normal part of their lovemaking. It doesn't interfere with their enjoyment, and it isn't a problem to them unless they think of it as one.

If you're tired, under stress, or have had a climax fairly recently, you may not feel the need to climax. In fact, you may not even be able to climax. This is simply your body's way of telling you that it doesn't need an orgasm at that moment. Trying to force it will only get you into trouble.

If you just relax and enjoy your lovemaking and don't worry whether you climax or not, you'll find that you may be able to continue with intercourse for a long time (to your partner's great pleasure). And, since you don't really need a climax, missing it won't cause you to feel sexually frustrated afterward.

In fact, if you don't climax you may keep your feeling of sexual stimulation so that you'll be able to have sex again later the same day. You won't have to wait as long as you ordinarily would before your sexual desire returns.

## "I'M NOT ALWAYS READY FOR SEX THE WAY I USED TO BE"

One of the myths that can get you into trouble is the one that claims a man should always be interested in having sex, that he should always be able to get aroused as long as he has a willing and attractive partner.

We don't expect that kind of response from a woman. While some men may inconsiderately expect their partners to be ready for sex at any time, most men and women realize that a woman usually needs a favorable emotional and physical environment in order to be sexually responsive and to become sexually aroused. She'll respond more readily, for instance, if she's in a relaxed frame of mind than if she's feeling stressed, tired, or worried.

Men, on the other hand, seem to feel that they should get turned on anytime their partner expresses willingness or interest. They may even be ashamed and embarrassed if they don't, or feel they are not fulfilling their masculine duty. This is very unrealistic, especially for men over forty.

As your need for climax gradually decreases in frequency, you will also discover that there are times when you're just not very sexually responsive—whether it's because you're worried or tired or just not feeling sexy for no particular reason. If this occurs, you may sometimes be able to get turned on with enough encouragement, but at other times it just may not be in the cards. If this occurs there's no reason for concern. Just help your partner climax manually or orally if she's already excited, and wait until the next time for yourself.

## IN SUMMARY

A lot of a man's feelings about how successful he is as a person depends on how successful he sees himself sexually. And most men, even those who really know better, have a nagging residue of some of these myths. Their unrealistic expectations, along with those of their partners, can produce much unnecessary heartache. These couples can open up their sex lives by relaxing their rigid preconceptions about lovemaking and enjoying a wider variety of sexual experience. The years after forty, when men and women have more leisure to explore sexually, are ideal for this.

# 6

# Overcoming Mental Obstacles to Really Good Sex

My practice has taught me that many men and women over forty would really like to enjoy sex more but find that some of their own ideas and thoughts block their enjoyment. They envy other men and women who appear to have free and open pleasure in their sexual lives, and they fear they may never be able to achieve it for themselves.

But it doesn't have to be this way. You can learn to be free sexually. You can learn to let yourself go, bypass distracting thoughts, reevaluate and shed old inhibitions, and change your preconceived ideas about lovemaking.

## OVERCOMING THOUGHTS THAT CAN DISTRACT YOU FROM FULLY ENJOYING SEX

Has the ability to enjoy, really enjoy, your lovemaking frequently been blocked by distracting thoughts that interfere, worry you, or undermine your arousal? Such thoughts can spoil an otherwise enjoyable lovemaking experience by preventing you from getting into a lovemaking mood or by ruining one after you're in it. They can block your excitement and prevent you from getting erect if you are a man; they can prevent you from becoming aroused, from lubricating, or from climaxing if you are a woman.

Each of us has experienced such mental interruptions at one time or another. But there *are* ways around them.

***Simple distractions*** can cause your mind to drift away from sensual feelings of lovemaking. They can lead to thoughts like

It's too hot (or cold) in here.

Are we making too much noise? Can anyone hear?

I have to go to the bathroom.

My arm is uncomfortable.

I wish the faucet would quit dripping.

What should we have for dinner?

What if the kids come home?

I have to get that report out tomorrow.

***Insecurity thoughts,*** especially worries about your own attractiveness, can make you preoccupied with your appearance or desirability instead of enjoying your partner's caresses:

My skin looks flabby.

I'm getting a pot belly.

I didn't shave my legs.

I wonder if I look fat.

He (or she) probably doesn't really enjoy caressing me.

I wonder if I smell bad.

*Concern about your sexual performance* can also get in the way of your enjoyment of sex and may even block successful functioning:

I don't think I'm going to get hard.

I'm not getting excited enough.

I don't think I will climax.

My penis isn't hard enough.

I must be taking too long.

He (or she) is probably getting tired of caressing me.

Worries about erection can often be self-fulfilling, with the resulting anxiety crowding out all your sensual feeling and actually preventing you from getting hard.

The same is true for women when it comes to arousal or climax. If your mind is filled with worries that you aren't getting excited or won't climax, those worries can bring about exactly what you fear.

*Putting sex last in your priorities* can become a major problem. Many people feel that they don't have time for sex. You may not think of it in exactly those terms, but you may always feel that there is something else "more important" that you should be doing. This may be because you haven't really been enjoying lovemaking or because you have been raised to feel that sex (and other pleasures) shouldn't be important to you or to your partner—especially now that you are older. In either case, it results in giving lovemaking a low priority in your life. This can lead to such distracting thoughts about time priorities during your lovemaking as these:

I don't have time for this.

I should be doing the laundry (or working on next week's proposal, or whatever).

I'm not going to get enough sleep.

Let's get it over with as fast as possible.

**Holding on to irritations and resentments** can be particularly destructive to your sexual enjoyment. Here we have:

I'm still angry at him (or her) for what happened earlier (or yesterday, or last week, or eight years ago).

I'm just having sex because he (or she) wants it.

He (or she) only acts nice and gives me attention when there's going to be sex.

**Worry about other problems** having to do with your business, your children, money or what you need to do tomorrow can make it very difficult for you to fully engage in satisfying lovemaking.

## STEPS TO A SOLUTION

How can you overcome these blocks to your own enjoyment? The first step is to clearly decide or confirm your decision that you really do want to enjoy lovemaking—for you, yourself. You may also want to partake in lovemaking for your partner's pleasure, but it's important to be clear in your own mind that having the pleasure, intimacy, and satisfaction of good lovemaking is something *you desire,* and that you don't want to spoil the experience with worry and resentments. Making this decision is an important, even crucial, step toward successful lovemaking.

**Reconsider priorities.** During the course of an ordinary day, you constantly order your own priorities, choosing to do certain things in place of others that would also be possible. It's important to choose lovemaking as a high priority in your life—more important than doing household chores or working on next month's financial report. The pleasure, warmth, and intimacy that you will get from satisfying lovemaking will mean more to you the next day, much more than getting an extra half-hour or forty-five minutes of sleep. It really will!

***Put aside resentments.*** If you are troubled by feelings of irritation and anger during lovemaking, you've probably found that it's difficult to set aside some of the hurts from the past as well as fresh arguments and disagreements. Indeed, some hurts are too big and too painful to overlook; only you can decide that. Realize, however, that holding on to your anger and resentment during lovemaking strongly interferes with your ability to respond sexually and to enjoy your lovemaking.

Perhaps it would help to keep your *long-range* goals in mind. Are you aiming for a relationship tomorrow, next week, or next month, in which you and your partner are still angry and unhappy with each other? Or would you like your relationship to be one in which you are sharing, intimate, and loving? If you really want this second kind of relationship, try to put aside your resentments while you are in bed. You'll have plenty of time to take them up in a neutral atmosphere later, if they still seem significant.

Good lovemaking has a wonderful, healing effect. Sometimes the petty irritations that were so important before lovemaking seem inconsequential after you've enjoyed a happy sexual experience.

***Focus your thoughts on your actual physical sensations.*** Some useful techniques can help you control the distractions, worry, and thoughts of insecurity that wander into your mind and get in the way of your sexual response.

The most simple, yet direct method is to *focus your thoughts on the physical sensations* you are receiving. Instead of dwelling on the roof needing repairs or worrying that you are not getting excited fast enough, *focus* on your actual physical feelings. Consider the feeling of smoothness, softness, or warmth of your partner's touch; the feel of that skin against yours, the warmth or roughness or coolness; if you are a man, the tingling feeling in your penis as your partner slides her hand up and down its shaft. Relaxing and concentrating on these things will help establish your own sensual mood.

**Tell each other about your feelings and sensations.** You can carry this technique one step further by relating what you are feeling, or by having your partner describe his or her sensations to you. This can be very sexually arousing, as well as a help in focusing your thoughts.

You might say, "Your hands feel really smooth and soft on my back," or "Your vagina feels really hot and wet around my penis." Or your partner might say, "Your tongue feels wet and velvety on my nipples," or "Your penis feels like it's filling up every bit of me." This type of passionate, sexually explicit dialogue can rapidly banish irrelevant thoughts.

**Fantasize.** Fantasy can be a very powerful way of focusing your thoughts on the sensual. Try imagining yourself in an especially sexy scene. You can fantasize about a previous encounter, about sex in a particular position or circumstance, or about how you would like to make love then and there. Or you can recall feelings you had in some particularly romantic or exciting lovemaking episode.

It can also be arousing to fantasize what the lovemaking feels like to your partner, and to imagine yourself in his or her place. For example, if you are a woman, imagine how exciting it must feel for your partner to have his penis sliding in and out of your vagina and to feel its velvety, warm wetness. If you are a man, imagine the sensations that your partner must have as she feels your penis inside her, filling her up. Sharing your partner's feelings like this will give you a whole new perspective.

*Help each other to overcome distractions.* If you are having trouble focusing or concentrating on lovemaking, learn to tell your partner and ask for his or her help. If you explain, for instance, that you can't concentrate because you're worried about some irrelevant concern, your partner may be able to help by talking sexily to you, by describing his or her sensations, or even by reassuring you.

Similarly, you can help your partner by giving positive feedback and reassurance. A woman whose partner has been worrying about his erections, for example, might say as she begins to feel him becoming aroused, "I can feel you getting excited—you're getting firm and warm right in my hands."

If you are a man and your partner is having trouble concentrating, you can describe the feeling of her nipples getting erect, her clitoris rolling under your finger, or the wetness and firmness of her vagina gripping your fingers.

Sometimes, if your partner is preoccupied or worried, making him or her laugh can be another very effective way to break the worry cycle and produce a more relaxed state.

Remember that you *can* control distracting and interfering thoughts. It's most important to make up your mind that you *do* want to enjoy lovemaking, you *don't* want to be blocked by resentments, by minor aggravations, or by worries, and that you *are* going to give lovemaking a high priority in your life.

## OVERCOMING THE INHIBITIONS THAT PREVENT YOU FROM BEING FREE

Preoccupation with leftover inhibitions from our antisexual upbringings can also get in the way of our full enjoyment of sex. These include all too many irrational rules about what's right and proper—making love at the "right" time and in the "right" place and in the "right" way. Worrying about everything being right and proper can, unfortunately, really limit your sexual horizons, give you a negative attitude about lovemaking in general, and be very damaging to your loving relationships.

Imagine that you're in the bathroom shaving. Your wife comes up behind you and rubs your chest and then slides her hand down and brushes it over your penis. Are you likely to say something like "I'm busy now"?

If you are a woman and you are in the middle of putting on your makeup and your husband comes up and squeezes your breasts, are you likely to say the same thing?

Stop and think: What does "busy" have to do with it anyway? How long will a penis caress or a breast squeeze take? Certainly no more than fifteen or thirty seconds. It won't hurt your shaving or your makeup to take a thirty-second break.

I think the concern that prevents many people from enjoying this kind of play is the feeling that sexual touching inevitably will lead to intercourse. There's no reason that should be so at all. If your partner caresses you while you're shaving, you could turn around and give her a hug and even rub her vaginal area with your hand, tell her how good her touches feel—and then go back and finish your shaving. She'll feel wonderfully rewarded for her efforts and you'll both have a nice glow.

You may decide sometimes to stop whatever you're doing and go ahead and make love right then and there on the bathroom counter, but it's certainly not required. You can exchange sexual touches and caresses in the same way that you give hugs, as a way of expressing your affection for each other and of telling each other that you're desirable and desired. Accepting a sexual caress with appreciation and enthusiasm doesn't commit you to intercourse.

It's the same if the two of you are in bed at the end of a long day and your husband leans over and licks one of your nipples. You could turn away with a lot of negative body language and remind him how tired you are, or on the other hand, you could tell him that the other nipple needs a lick too. You could then give him a big hug and tell him how much you appreciated his licks but that you're really exhausted and ready for sleep.

What a difference there'll be in the way the two of you go to sleep! The first response is likely to project a feeling of annoyance and being pressured on your part and produce a feeling of being rejected and hurt on your partner's. The second response may well allow you both to feel appreciated, content, and loved. And who knows—you may even decide you aren't as tired as you thought and go ahead and enjoy lovemaking anyway, even if it's just a little appetizer of the kind described in chapter 13.

If your partner suggests making love leaning over the bathroom counter or the bed or sitting in a chair, do you find yourself reacting with an immediate negative response without even thinking? Do you tend to feel that making love in different positions or in different ways is somehow "not nice" or even perverted?

Stop and think! Why in the world should the position that you're lying or standing in when the penis goes into the vagina have anything to do with rightness or wrongness or with morality in any way? Don't restrict your lovemaking unnecessarily. Allow yourself the adventure. Experiment with all the myriad positions and types of lovemaking that you and your partner might enjoy.

If you've just finished a leisurely Sunday breakfast alone together and your partner slips her hand inside your pajamas, are you likely to take her hand away and say "not here" or "not now"? But *why not* here? And *why not* now? Why should it be that sexual touching is allowed only in one room of your house, the bedroom? Whoever said that sexual touching was appropriate at night in bed but not in the morning after breakfast? Yet many of us harbor such leftover feelings of what's proper and what's not.

When you find yourself starting to get these "not here, not now" feelings, try to examine them yourself. Is there anything *really* wrong with *right here* and *right now?* Sexual touching or even making love in unexpected places and times can kindle a new feeling of sexual interest and inspire vitality in your lovemaking. It can add variety and excitement and a feeling of being deliciously daring.

Try to get away from all those concerns and negative messages about sex. Quit worrying about what your mother or your friends would think if they knew that you were making love in broad daylight right here on the dining room table. When and where it's appropriate for you and your partner to make love privately is your own decision— whether it's in the morning, in the dining room, or on the sofa, if you so desire.

Leave yourselves open to experiment and allow yourself to give or receive sexual touches at any time without feeling annoyed or irritated. Getting your mental obstacles out of the way will keep you from depriving yourself of good feelings of pleasure, warmth, being loved, and knowing that your partner desires you.

# 7

# Sexual Variety: Romance and Sensual Adventures

For too many older couples, lovemaking has lost its spontaneity. They find themselves always making love in the same way, in the same place, at the same time. It's usually in bed, in the dark, before going to sleep, and with no romantic atmosphere whatsoever.

If this is the way your lovemaking is going, you may be justified in feeling that it's becoming dull and boring. Making love in romantic settings may sound fine for someone else but hard to imagine for *yourself*—something like sky diving or traveling to Tahiti. If your sex life has gotten into this rut, try using this chapter to help yourself break out of it.

Some of these suggestions may seem too romantic or "silly" to you at first, maybe all right for "young lovers" but not for you. That's a mistake! Give romance a chance. You'll find that it can be fun and exciting once you get past your initial awkwardness. There is no rule that you have to give up romance and excitement at any age.

## AN AFTERNOON DELIGHT

Instead of always making love at night, when one or both
of you may be tired, try an "afternoon delight." You may
be able to find time on the weekend, schedule some time off
on a workday, take a long lunch hour, or use some other
strategy. It may be more exciting if it's at a time when you
wouldn't ordinarily be together.

Plan your afternoon dalliance at a time when you won't
be disturbed. Unplug the phone. Perhaps this might be the
time for lovemaking in or near the sunlight streaming in
from your window. Prepare your own little romantic island
by spreading a quilt, light mattress, or furry rug on the floor
in some interesting corner of your home.

Gather some large pillows for added comfort if you
have them, and, weather and privacy permitting, open your
windows to allow a warm, soft breeze to blow on you.

Pick some music that you both enjoy. It's best to use
music without interruptions—stacked records, tape, a radio
station without commercial breaks.

To please your other senses for your afternoon adventure, arrange some fresh fruit, such as berries, grapes, orange
slices, or cut melon, as well as your favorite cheese nearby.
Select a light white wine or a sparkling water.

Start off by relaxing on your romantic island. Caress
each other lightly and tenderly; there's no need to rush. Stop
and feed each other a grape or two. Try stroking the fruit
along your partner's cheek or lips. This can be very sensual
and exciting. Sip your wine and continue to enjoy your
sensual adventure with whatever style of lovemaking you
choose.

## A FLORAL BOUQUET

This adventure was a favorite of Jane F., who told me she
thought any woman would love it. I think almost any man

would too. It can take place anytime or anyplace, although daylight is best, to fully benefit from the pleasurable visual effects.

The setting requires a bouquet of flowers and a large, attractive bowl. Choose blooms with lots of soft petals and a variety of colors—daisies, carnations, roses, and others. Gently pull the petals off the flowers until the bowl is full of a medley of different hues.

Start off by sprinkling flower petals over your partner's closed eyes, face, body, and genital area. Make attractive designs, and let your partner's nipples poke through. Stroke his or her face and nipples with velvety rose petals, alternating with caresses. Gently slide the soft, silky petals around your partner's body, caressing through the satiny feel of the flowers.

If the two of you desire, you can switch places. Give your partner the pleasure of heaping the petals on you and caressing you through them. Then go ahead and make love in your bed full of flower petals. It will be an experience you won't forget.

## A BUBBLE BATH FOR TWO

Playing in a sensual bubble bath is a wonderful prelude to lovemaking. You may never have tried taking a bubble bath together, or you may have when you were younger but not in recent years.

A romantic atmosphere will help. Your bathroom will feel different if you use candles instead of the usual harsh, white bathroom light. Arrange several candles around the area for flickering light. You might like to have some wine, juice, or other drink available. Grapes or orange slices are also good and can be handled with wet hands.

Run the bath with a generous supply of bubbles and invite your partner to join you. You may be concerned that your tub will be too small for both of you, but give it a try. If there isn't enough room to sit facing each other, you can sit bobsled style, one behind the other.

Enjoy the soothing, creamy feel of the bubbles and play with them while washing each other, caressing and touching. When you've had enough, towel each other dry. Use large, luxurious bath towels, if you have them. There is something very delicious about taking care of each other so nicely.

If your skin feels a little dry after the bath, take the opportunity to enjoy applying body lotion, oil, or moisturizer to each other as well.

A bubble bath together can be enjoyed simply for its own sake, or it can serve as a relaxing introduction to love-making.

## THE ROMANTIC BREAKFAST

You'll have to plan ahead for this gourmet feast, gathering some of the ingredients in advance. Use a weekend morning when you'll be at home, undisturbed, with plenty of time to spend. You won't want to be hurrying.

Set the table for two, using your favorite place settings. This is an excellent time for your best china, silver, and linen napkins. A small bouquet of flowers or even just a single rose in a bud vase will add a loving touch.

Dress for breakfast as the two of you feel comfortable. On a warm summer day, some couples I've known like to dine in the nude or seminude. On the other hand, you might feel more comfortable in an attractive robe or have fun dressing up in formal clothes.

You might start your breakfast by sipping a delicious Mimosa Breeze, made with half orange juice and half champagne and with grenadine or maraschino cherry syrup added to taste (a carbonated lemon-lime drink can be substituted for the champagne). Garnish with a sprig of fresh mint, and serve with a cocktail straw.

Start a lighter menu with a fresh-fruit plate, and add a pastry and perhaps an egg dish. Another menu might include croissants and a small black- or red-caviar omelette capped with sour cream, a perfect romantic breakfast. Classical music or soft mood music might best complement the setting.

After the meal, it's back to bed to complete a leisurely morning. If you have privacy, open your blinds and let the sun shine in, or enjoy the sound of rain pattering on your windows.

Continue your sensual pleasure with a light, titillating backrub. Enjoy some mutual stroking and caressing, interspersed with a few more sips of your Mimosa Breeze, and perhaps feed each other some seedless grapes or strawberries saved from your fruit plate. Proceed with lovemaking in whatever fashion seems right at the moment.

## FEATHERING

Feathers are made for caressing. They are light, gentle, and soft, and feather caresses can be especially sensual and titillating.

Feathering is a leisurely pastime, so choose an occasion when the two of you are unhurried, warm, and comfortable. Some slow, relaxed music would fit the mood.

If possible, find three or four feathers of different sizes and consistencies. If not, a new, unused feather duster or two will do. Feathers have their own personalities: stiffer, pointed ones are best for tickling with the tip or edge, while softer, flowing ones are for gentle caresses.

With your partner on his or her back, start with soft, fluttery movements around the cheeks and eyelashes. You can stroke along your partner's cheeks with the side of the feather or tickle behind the ears with the tip of one.

Gradually move down to the chest and use flowing feather caresses to gently stroke the nipples. Men as well as women will enjoy this.

Continue down your partner's thighs and abdomen. Tickling in the crease of the thighs and stroking movements on the inner thigh can be very stimulating. Let your imagination run wild.

Using the feathers in this way can wonderfully tantalize your partner. You can find sensitive places on the back of the neck and in the cleavage of the backside, behind the knees and under the arms.

After a while, switch places so your partner can feather you. It's just as much fun to receive as to give, you'll find, and it will help you both to feel luxurious and pampered. It's a wonderful preparation for lovemaking.

## LOVEMAKING WITH WARMED OIL

On cold winter nights few experiences are as sensuous as giving your partner a soft massage with warmed oil. This special treat tends to be most attractive when it's cold and wintery outside, but warm and toasty inside.

Prepare your room by creating a warm atmosphere. Candlelight's soft, flickering glow contributes to an overall sensual mood when you're giving a massage. A nice fire is a wonderful alternative. Add some soft music that you both enjoy. Some scented massage oils are made especially for oil rubs, but a kitchen oil such as corn oil or safflower oil will do as well.

Get ready by putting about a half cup of oil in a small bottle with a cap or stopper. A plastic bottle with a flip-top spout has advantages because you don't have to keep it upright; you can simply lay it down in your bed.

Warm the oil by placing the bottle in a sink full of hot water. Be sure to test the temperature of the oil before using it, though—and don't heat it on a stove or in a microwave, as oil quickly gets very hot.

When the oil is comfortably warm, it's time to begin. (As I discuss the lovemaking in the next few pages I will first address a man caressing his partner and then address the woman, but there's no particular reason for this order. Either partner can go first and the exercise will be equally enjoyable.)

To him: Have your partner lie on her stomach while you sit alongside her and slide your fingers lightly up and down her back. Feel the texture of her skin, while she concentrates on the feel of your fingertips. Then pour a small amount of the warmed oil in the small of her back. Spread it out with your hand in ever-widening circles. Add more as you need to. Notice the changes in texture and sensation as oiled skin becomes smooth and silky. Your strokes and caresses will slide liquidly. Notice how the oil feels warm at first, but then has liquid coolness.

Try a variety of different touches. Use swirls, short strokes, and long strokes all up and down her back, and then light caresses with the tips of your fingers. Let your partner tell you what the caressing feels like. Ask what about your massage feels best. Be slow and leisurely, take your time. Add a little more warm oil from time to time to keep the warmth and the silky feeling.

Now pour a small amount of oil on her buttocks and the back of her thighs, and let your hands teasingly play with these more sexually sensitive areas. Then spread her legs a little, cup a little of the warm oil in your hands, and, after making sure that it's not too warm, apply it gently to her vulva.

Lubricating her vaginal area with the warm oil will add to her arousal as well as yours. The inside of her vaginal lips and her vaginal opening will be soft and warm, silky and wet. You can make small, circular movements with one or two fingers inside her vaginal lips and around her clitoris while your other hand continues to slide up and down her back. This can provide her a most enjoyable combination— enjoying a backrub and having her genital area stimulated at the same time. Then reach between her legs and slide your hand through her wet vulval area. It will feel delightfully velvety with the oil.

Switch hands or take a break by caressing her back and

sides again. Then put some more oil in your hand and return to her genital area.

To her: You may already be quite aroused, but if the two of you can wait, you may wish to caress your partner with the oil in the same way. You can begin by giving him a back massage, stroking his buttocks and between his legs. Or just start by having him turn over on his back while you help him get hard by caressing his penis and scrotum with the warm oil. You'll enjoy sliding your hands up and down his wet penis, and he'll think it's great. It will give him a double sensation if you cup his scrotum in one hand while you stroke his penis with the other. You can also use your mouth and tongue to help get him fully aroused and hard (ingesting small amounts of corn oil or safflower oil is harmless, of course).

Once you are both aroused and your partner is hard, you'll enjoy straddling him and sliding his penis into your vagina. After playing in this position for a while, roll over; with the fronts of your bodies slippery with oil, intercourse in a face-to-face position will have an added dimension as your entire bodies slide against each other. You will especially enjoy the feeling of your partner's chest sliding against your breasts as his penis thrusts in and out of your vagina.

Making love with warm oil is an experience you can enjoy and come back to over and over again. It will be a very pleasurable addition to your lovemaking variety and skills.

## LOVEMAKING WITH MIRRORS

Making love in front of a mirror can add to your feelings of intimacy and arousal while you share the stimulation of seeing your own sexual responses.

If you'd like to try this interesting variation, we suggest you prepare a suitable atmosphere in advance. A couple of candles set at the far ends of a mirror and reflecting in it can create a beautiful setting. And as always, some soft music will complement the mood.

A mirror across the room is probably too far away. If you're ten feet from the mirror, your image seems twenty feet away. If you have to strain to see yourself, you've lost the effect.

More than likely, your house won't have a movable mirror, so consider moving your bed in front of a fixed mirror to experiment. If this isn't convenient, try making love in front of one of the large mirrors found over bathroom counters, dressing tables, or a chest of drawers. You might want to place a pillow or two on the countertop to lean on for comfort.

Begin by standing together in the nude in front of the mirror. Caress your partner and cup her breasts in your hands while you both enjoy the view of your bodies with the candlelight flickering on you. Lubricate her vaginal area with a little warm lovemaking oil. Your partner can help you to get hard by playing with your penis and applying some oil to it—and she may enjoy licking your penis or sucking on it while you both watch. Seeing your bodies in the candlelight and watching the preparation can build a delicious sexual tension for both of you.

Let your partner lean forward over the counter or dressing table and rest her arms and head on a pillow for comfort. As you stand behind her, caress her buttocks and labia and then spread her vaginal lips and run your fingers softly around her vaginal opening and over her clitoris. Slide your penis inside her and place your hand on her hips to guide your movements while you both enjoy watching your bodies move in rhythm to the music. You'll be surprised at how arousing this can be.

If the two of you shift around slightly to stand at an angle to the mirror, you'll get a good view of each other and your body movements, which will look especially attractive in the flickering candlelight. Standing sideways to the mirror like this will give your partner a better view. She may even be able to see your penis sliding in and out of her vagina. If by any chance you have a second mirror that you can set at an angle (on the bathroom door, for instance), you'll be able to observe your lovemaking from several different directions.

Many people find it extraordinarily stimulating to watch themselves in a mirror and see the beauty of their bodies in action. Others feel that it's not as pleasurable as the "close in bed" atmosphere that they are accustomed to in lovemaking. If you've never tried it, I suggest you do so at least once—if only to discover that you really look surprisingly attractive during sex.

## THE EXTENDED BREAST CARESS

Caressing your partner's breasts can be a prelude to intercourse, or it can be a lovemaking art-form all its own. It can vary from a little "good morning" lick of her nipple to an extended erotic caress. It can be very sexually exciting, or else soothing and relaxing, depending on the mood and circumstances.

To begin, choose a time when you are at leisure and unhurried. Gradually start making love to one of your partner's breasts as you lie alongside her. I say "making love" to one of her breasts, because that's what you will do. You'll give that breast the most wonderfully complete, loving attention it's ever had.

Start by gently licking around the base of her breast, and with gradual swirls of your tongue work your way toward her nipple. Tease a little by playing near her nipple with your tongue, retreating and returning to it.

As your partner's nipples become erect and seem to reach out for your caress, try the lightest of touches—with a cotton ball, Q-tip, feather, or filmy, smooth material. Blow on her nipple and touch it ever so lightly with the tip of your tongue.

Watch the nipple react as you flick it with your tongue, suck on it gently, or bathe it softly with your open lips or the fullness of your soft tongue. Dip a little wine or your favorite after-dinner liqueur on the nipple with a cotton ball or your finger and lick it off. Try a lovemaking oil like Kama Sutra, which warms the skin as you blow on it or touch it with your tongue. After the coolness of the alcohol, this will create another pleasant sensation for your partner, and it will taste interesting for you as well.

Cup her breast with both of your hands and bring her nipple up to your mouth as you continue to bathe it with your tongue. Try different kinds of strokes, licking softly over the nipple, taking it entirely in your mouth and rolling it with your tongue, or making swirling movements around it. Run the erect nipple between your lips or gently between your fingers. Cup one hand over it and let it tickle your palm.

You may find that you're giving attention to your partner's breast for twenty to thirty minutes. It can be a really ecstatic experience for her, especially if she knows that you're enjoying it too. In fact, the other breast may get jealous, and you may get an earnest request to do the same on the other side—thereby doubling the fun for both of you.

This breast stimulation can be an end in itself. You can give your partner a nipple bath with your tongue before dropping off to sleep, or you can waken her in the morning with some tantalizing little nipple licks.

On the other hand, you can continue stimulating her breasts with your tongue and lips while one of your fingers slips into her vulval opening. Some lovemaking oil or lubricant will add to her wetness, and you can carry on giving your partner double stimulation—caressing her clitoris and nipple at the same time—until you finish by having intercourse, a wonderful conclusion to this delightful adventure.

# A WAY TO ADD
# FLAVOR TO YOUR LOVEMAKING

For a treat that can add variety to your lovemaking at any time, consider adding some ordinary food flavorings to your edible lovemaking oils—peppermint, almond, or vanilla, for instance.

Chocolate-cherry is a special favorite. It tastes delicious on nipples, penis, and vulva, and it has the rich flavor and aroma of an after-dinner liqueur or one of those luscious chocolate-covered cherry candies.

Let your imagination go. If you have a sweet tooth, you'll be that much more inspired to experiment with different flavors, which will impart a wonderful taste treat along with the experience of the sight, sound, and touch of your partner.

# AND A FINAL HINT

Do you find yourself thinking about lovemaking when you get up, feeling sexual tingling in the morning, joking with your friends or business associates about sex during the day, looking forward to it at dinner—but then all too often feeling, as you get in bed late at night, that your body is tired and ready for sleep and desire has disappeared?

As the years have gone by, you've probably noticed that you simply tire out earlier in the evening, while lovemaking continues to require energy, creativity, and enthusiasm. If late at night, after the evening news, is when you usually plan your sex life, just plain weariness can often cause disappointment and take most of the enjoyment out of it. By evening you're likely to be preoccupied with the concerns, annoyances, and anxieties of the day, and this stress, as well as simple fatigue, makes the transition to a sexual mood a difficult one.

Lovemaking in the morning gives you the opportunity to make love when your body is rested and your mind is fresh and clear. It has real advantages for men and women over forty, and it can make sex a pleasure instead of a chore.

There will be some days when you simply don't have the opportunity to lie in bed for any length of time. On other occasions, however, you may be able to arrange for leisurely awakening and the luxury of morning lovemaking. You can proceed imperceptibly from closeness and touching during sleep to gradual cuddling, hugging, and caressing. As your lovemaking begins, you may feel extremely sensuous, close, and intimate, as if in the continuation of a pleasant dream.

Even on mornings when you have to arise fairly early, you can still enjoy a sensual "appetizer" together. A few minutes of intimate loveplay can help establish a feeling of excitement and closeness that lasts throughout the day. There is no need for either of you to climax. It can just be a quick reminder of your love and affection for each other.

# 8

# Understanding Your Older Man

If you are a woman whose partner is experiencing some of the sexual changes of aging, there are ways in which you can help him, as well as yourself, to enjoy sex more fully. By assisting him in achieving and maintaining firmer erections during lovemaking, you will also be reassuring him of how much you care for him at a time when he may be experiencing great insecurity about his attractiveness and masculinity, as well as his sexual performance.

Anxiety about performance can turn a man's natural changes of aging into real sexual dysfunction. If your partner's sexual changes are compounded by medical conditions that interfere with his erection, you may not be able to entirely overcome these problems yourself. You will, however, certainly be able to alleviate whatever part of his problem is caused by worry over his sexual performance and his need for loving sexual stimulation.

Now that your partner is forty or older, he no longer has the same sexual response as when he was twenty. As a very young man, his erection drive was so strong that he could usually perform under the least conducive of conditions. He could get erect in awkward, cramped positions in the back seat of a car. He could still get erect after a dozen beers. He would even manage to get erect when you didn't want sex and weren't responsive at all.

If you think back on those years when your partner got hard just seeing you in the nude or thinking about the two of you making love, it's tempting to blame yourself and wonder, *Has he lost interest in me? Is he bored with me?* or even *Is he having an affair with someone else?*

Of course, any of these developments may be true, but the fact that he's no longer springing to erection just seeing you undressed isn't necessarily a manifestation of it. He may very well still find you attractive and care deeply about you. It's simply a natural result of aging. And just as your partner's eyes may now need some help from eyeglasses, his penis needs some help with *direct physical stimulation* from you.

## HE MAY SEEM TO HAVE LOST INTEREST IN SEX

A common complaint I've encountered in my practice treating sexual dysfunctions is "He doesn't seem interested in sex anymore." Women often report that they and their partners are having sexual relations quite infrequently—once in two weeks, once a month, even less than that. These women want to have sex more frequently, but they say they can't get their partners interested.

In these circumstances it often turns out that the woman's partner hasn't really lost interest in sex at all. The real problem is that he's become insecure about his erection ability and worried about his sexual performance. He's afraid to initiate sex because he's worried that he won't be able to get hard if he does.

## HOW PERFORMANCE ANXIETY
## CAN AFFECT HIS SEX LIFE

It's astounding, the amount of apprehension and worry your partner may develop if he's had a few repeated episodes of difficulty.

Erection problems are often worsened by this performance anxiety, and the two may work together to create a vicious circle. Your partner may start feeling apprehension before the lovemaking even starts. The more anxiety he has, and the more he mentally watches himself to see if he's getting hard, the more trouble he'll actually have and the more difficult it will be for him not to worry the next time.

## WOMEN HAVE A BIG
## ADVANTAGE IN LOVEMAKING

Women are used to fluctuation in their own level of excitement. They know that they may become very aroused during lovemaking on some occasions and not quite as excited on others, and that excitement levels may vary during the lovemaking sessions themselves. Women generally tend to take this fluctuation for granted and don't react with much concern if they are less responsive at one particular time. For this reason, it may be hard for you, as a woman, to understand why your male partner gets so upset when he's less responsive and has difficulty getting an erection.

You have a big advantage being a woman. You can begin lovemaking and proceed to intercourse even if you're preoccupied, worried, or not very excited. You can start even if you're not lubricated. It may not be very satisfactory to you, but you *can* do it if you want to—if, for instance, you want to please your partner, even though you aren't feeling sexy yourself. You may then become more excited once you've begun.

On the other hand, if your partner is worried or preoccupied, he probably won't be able to get an erection to begin with. And if he can't get erect, he is simply unable to go ahead with intercourse.

Try to imagine how he feels: He wants very much to get an erection and feels that you'll be disappointed if he doesn't. He probably feels that an erection is necessary for lovemaking (although it's not), yet he himself has no control over it. He can't make himself get hard, anymore than you can make yourself get wet vaginally.

In fact, vaginal lubrication for a woman is in many ways the equivalent of getting erect for a man. It is a natural response to sexual stimulation, when it's not blocked by anxiety or other negative emotions. Imagine if you *had* to get wet in order to have intercourse! There isn't any way to *make* yourself lubricate, of course. The harder you "tried," the more trouble you'd be likely to have. And if you couldn't get wet on one occasion, you would probably worry even more the next time.

If that sounds nightmarish to you, realize that older men *often* feel under that kind of pressure to perform. The stress is sometimes so bad that they just give up on sex completely rather than endure any more embarrassment or feelings of failure.

## IT'S NOT BECAUSE HE DOESN'T FIND YOU ATTRACTIVE

As we mentioned before, your partner's difficulty in becoming aroused most probably has nothing to do with any lack of sexual interest in you, but instead reflects that his body is now simply less spontaneous in translating sexual interest into an erection. His penis now requires stroking in order to get hard.

Realizing and accepting this will enable you to put aside any feelings of resentment or insecurity and allow you to be the caring, helping, and loving sexual partner that you

would like to be. Remember, you have a choice: you can
ignore his needs and possibly create a wall or barrier between the two of you, or you can assist him and greatly add
to the intimacy, warmth, and love of your relationship.

## COOPERATION AND
## UNDERSTANDING ARE CRUCIAL

Often in my practice I may see two older men with the same
potential sexual ability. One of them is functioning well and
enjoying a satisfying and successful sexual life. The other
thinks that he's impotent, or partly impotent, and is frustrated and unhappy. The primary difference between them
may be that the first man has a cooperative, understanding
partner who cheerfully helps him to function, while the
second man's partner is uncooperative and negative about
sex. This is no exaggeration; a man's partner can easily make
that much difference.

Your attitude will be very important to your mutual
success in maintaining a healthy sex life. It's important to
curb irritation or resentment if your partner has sexual difficulties. Demanding that your partner get an erection in order
to make love will only put additional performance pressure
on him, which will make him even less likely to function in
the way that you desire.

## ALLOW YOUR PARTNER TO BE A GOOD
## LOVER EVEN WITHOUT AN ERECTION

If your partner has trouble on a particular occasion, it will
work much better if you cheerfully accept having him pleasure you manually or orally. This will achieve a much better
result than insisting on intercourse as your exclusive means
of sexual gratification. It will give your partner the feeling
that he can satisfy you and be a good lover whether or not

his penis gets hard. This will decrease his anxiety and his pressure for performance, and it will probably make it easier for him to get hard without worry the next time you make love.

Many a man whom I've seen in my practice with erection problems has told me that his partner won't allow him to bring her to climax by manual or oral means if he can't get hard. Sometimes it's because she thinks he doesn't really want to. Other women feel, misguidedly, that "it's not natural" or confuse sexual stimulation by their partner with masturbation, which of course usually refers to self-stimulation.

It's really a mistake to turn down your partner's attempts to please you manually. In doing so, you're giving him a message that the only way he can *really* please you is by getting hard, and that message puts a great deal of pressure on him.

Now that your partner's erection mechanism is more fragile, your cooperation and help will be very important. And there is *nothing* that will make an older man more appreciative than having a partner who helps to restore his erection ability. I'll explore more about how you can help your partner in the next chapter.

# 9

# How to Help Your Man Get Firm Erections

## SETTING THE STAGE

If your partner is like many older men, he will definitely be able to get erect when conditions are favorable, but he may have difficulty when they're not. Therefore, it can help if the two of you try to establish a sensual, nondistracting environment. You can do this by dimming the lights, adding soft music, and disconnecting the telephone, for example.

It's a mistake to make love only late at night, when you're both fatigued. Your partner will probably get erect more easily when you are both rested in the morning. Midafternoon on a relaxed weekend is another good time. Lovemaking when your partner is under high stress or when both of you are feeling pressured may result in temporary erection difficulties. It may take a little while for your partner to get erect under the best of circumstances. Allow adequate time whenever possible so that neither of you feel rushed.

It's a good idea to have a lubricant on hand. Extra lubrication can be a valuable aid for penetration when your partner's erection isn't as fully hard as you both might wish. (A simple kitchen oil like corn oil or safflower oil will do.)

## STARTING LOVEMAKING

It's important that you both realize that it isn't necessary to have an erection before starting lovemaking—only the desire to make love.

Many couples begin lovemaking with simultaneous hugging, caressing, and petting. However, it's often helpful to *take turns* in caressing each other. Your partner may sometimes want to bring you to a climax with manual or oral petting even before you start caressing him. Helping you climax may reassure him that he can satisfy you and may allow him to be less anxious about getting hard. Men often worry a great deal about their sexual function, and worrying about getting hard enough to satisfy you can certainly interfere with his getting erect.

When you start to caress him, let him know that it's his turn to relax and enjoy. Remind him that he doesn't need to worry about getting hard because you really enjoy making love with him and he can give you lots of sexual pleasure, whether or not he gets an erection on this particular occasion.

Assuming that your lover has had difficulty with erections, you can begin your arousal of him by having him lie on his stomach and giving him a gentle overall body massage to help him relax. This can be accompanied by stroking over his buttocks and sliding your hand gently between his legs to stroke the back of his scrotum and the base of his penis from behind.

When your partner rolls over on his back, continue with light stroking movements between his thighs and along his scrotum and penis. Use very light touches on his scrotum, because the testicles are very sensitive.

The most sexually sensitive places for a man are usually the underside of his penis and the ridge below the head of his penis (the *coronal ridge*). The little indentation of that ridge on the underside of the penis is called the *frenulum* and is extra-sensitive. If the man is uncircumcised, the foreskin will retract as he becomes erect and the head of his penis, which will be exposed, will be especially sensitive.

## CARING AND TENDER CARESSES

Approach caressing with an artistic and creative attitude. You want to do the best, most sensual, most imaginative job possible. Being caring and tender, however, is most important of all. Softly stroke and caress your partner's inner thighs, slip the tips of your fingers lightly along the hairs of his scrotum, and slide your fingertips or your tongue down the underside of the shaft of his penis. Softly cup his scrotum in your hand as you stroke his penis with your other hand.

Now begin sliding your hand up and down the whole shaft of your partner's penis, swirling or slipping over and around the coronal ridge. A gentle rhythmic pulling movement on the shaft and head of his penis will also help him to get hard. You can do this either with your hand or with your mouth.

Use your imagination to picture what your partner would enjoy, and ask him to give you feedback and let you know what excites him. Remember, too, that just as you may vary from day to day in what touches feel just right to you, the same may be true for him.

## STIMULATE HIS PENIS
## WITH LUBRICATING OIL

Using oil on your partner's penis will feel very sensuous to him, as if you were applying suntan oil or baby oil. Sometimes oil will feel cool if applied directly from the bottle, so you might warm it in your hands first. Or, as suggested in chapter 7, place the container in some hot water in your sink. The oil will help your hands slide up and down without irritating his penis. The wet, slippery sensation will create a feeling similar to the one he gets when his penis is inside your vagina.

Be gentle but firm when playing with your partner's penis. After you have applied oil, you can try different kinds of stimulation, such as sliding the penis between the palms of your hands laid flat, as if you were rolling a stick or a piece of dough. You can use one hand to hold the base of the shaft while you slide the other up and down over the coronal ridge. You might try using just the tips of your fingers. Remember to ask your partner what kinds of touches he likes best.

Many men find that long strokes up and down the shaft of the penis are important in helping it to get hard, while touches around the exquisitely sensitive ridge (equivalent, perhaps, to your clitoris) help bring him to climax. There is a tremendous overlap, however, between the two kinds of sensations, either of which may work best at different times.

Most older men also find that oral stimulation of the penis is especially valuable in helping them get hard. There will be more about this in the next chapter.

## HIS NIPPLES MAY BE ESPECIALLY SENSITIVE

Two important areas of a man's body that are often overlooked are his nipples. You can lick your partner's nipples or touch them with your fingertips while you're simultaneously stroking his penis. They can be quite sensitive—even as sensitive as yours. Your partner may tell you that the sensation goes right from his nipple to the tip of his penis, if you are stroking his penis at the same time.

Nipple stimulation can be especially important as an aid to ejaculation. If, on some occasions, he finds that he just can't climax during intercourse or even during manual stimulation, lightly flicking or pinching his nipples at the same time may provide the necessary extra stimulation that he needs.

## WHAT IF HE
## CONTINUES TO BE ANXIOUS?

Don't get discouraged if your partner doesn't get erect in the first minute or two. He may be dealing with a lot of anxiety and also may be wondering how you feel about caressing him. Before he can relax enough to let an erection happen, he needs to feel secure and confident in you, to realize that you enjoy making love to him, and to know that you won't be angry if he fails to get erect.

If he continues to worry or seems preoccupied with anxiety, try to distract him with sexual thoughts. Get him to talk to you and tell you what your hands and mouth feel like on his penis, or have him recall a specifically exciting lovemaking episode the two of you enjoyed together. Tell him to describe it to you in detail. This will help him focus his attention sexually.

As an alternative, you might talk to him while you stroke him. Tell him what his penis feels like, how good it feels to you, or what its texture is like when you stroke it or lick it and feel it growing. Another choice would be to tell him your favorite sex fantasy or reminisce about a particularly exciting lovemaking session and what it felt like for you. If he concentrates on what you're saying, it will certainly take his mind off worrying, and this will allow your sexual stimulation to do its job and make him hard.

When you find a method of stimulation that works, remember it for the next time he has difficulty. Using a method that he knows has worked before will give him more confidence, both in your ability to help him and in his own ability to get hard.

## WHAT IF HIS ERECTION GOES DOWN?

In most cases, the kinds of caressing that we have described above will enable your partner to have a good erection, provided he doesn't have a medical problem. Now that your partner is over forty, however, it may take him some time before he can climax, and his erection itself may not last that long. In fact, his erection may go down at perplexing and sometimes inexplicable times—such as right in the middle of intercourse.

When your partner loses his erection, he may tend to get discouraged and disgusted with himself and feel humiliated. He may also believe that he can't get hard again once his first erection is gone. Therefore, if your partner has been having trouble with maintaining his erection, he may hurry to try to use it as soon as he gets hard. This will add to his anxiety and may cause him to lose his erection even more quickly.

There is really no need for the momentary loss of erection to be a problem. It depends entirely on how the two of you deal with it. There is no earthly reason why one erection has to last for the whole time of lovemaking. If your partner loses his first erection, he can have a second or third later in that lovemaking episode, especially if you help him regain it.

## USE THE TEASING
## TECHNIQUE TO BUILD HIS CONFIDENCE

An easy technique—one that is frequently used in sexual therapy—can help you build your partner's confidence and assist him in dealing with occasional loss of erection. It's called the Teasing Technique, and here's how it works:

Start by agreeing beforehand that you won't have intercourse during this exercise—even if your partner gets the world's hardest erection. This will ease performance pressure. He won't have to worry that he's not going to get hard enough to penetrate, since you won't be going on to intercourse anyway. When he does start to get hard, he won't be preoccupied, worrying that he may lose his erection before he can complete the lovemaking.

Let your partner lie back and relax. Gradually run your fingertips around his penis. Lubricate it with your favorite lovemaking oil or other lubricant. Then gently stroke his penis with your hands or lick and pull it with your lips, as I described earlier in the chapter. Continue until your partner gets erect.

When he does, keep playing with his penis but don't bring him to a climax and don't go on to intercourse. Then, after a little while, *just stop and let his erection go back down!* This may seem like a strange thing to do, but you're going to help him get and lose his erection several times today.

In the past, when he was worried about keeping his erection, he may have lost it easily. Now, when you want it to go down, it may be obstinate and refuse. In this case, it's okay to play around a little—tickle him, sprinkle water on his penis, make him laugh. Then, when his erection has finally gone down, you can return and get him aroused again or else take a break and let him caress you.

After a brief rest, help him to get hard again, and then let his erection go down again. Repeat this process a few times, with short breaks in between. You will both be amazed at how many times he can get erect, as long as he hasn't reached a climax.

When you are ready to conclude your lovemaking, decide whether or not you will bring him to a climax with oral or manual stimulation. He may be happy just with the repeated excitation and wish to save his climax for a subsequent lovemaking experience later that day or the next, when the two of you may wish to have full intercourse. Your own climax can come either before or after his.

The series of erections that you help your partner get and then lose in one lovemaking episode will help him realize that losing his erection isn't the end of the world. He'll know that he has the capacity for many erections, and that at his age having erections come and go is just a natural part of the lovemaking process, not any kind of crisis.

Repeat the Teasing Technique at least once a week for three or four weeks to build his confidence. Do this exercise in addition to your regular lovemaking. After a while, if your partner loses his erection during intercourse, he'll *know* that you can help him to get it back, most of the time, lovingly and without complaint. This reassurance will help him to function as well as he possibly can. There will inevitably be an occasional time when his erection won't come back, no matter what. Don't try to force it. There's always another time!

Most older men will respond very well to the simple, helpful methods described in these last two chapters. If, however, in spite of your best efforts, your partner's erection problems persist, there are two possible explanations. The first is that he may have a medical problem due to illness, medication side-effects, lack of hormones, vascular insufficiency, or other physical difficulties that I will examine in subsequent chapters. In this case, he will need a medical evaluation. The other possibility is that there is nothing physically wrong but a great deal of anxiety about his sexual functioning that hasn't yet been eliminated by your reassurance and caressing.

It's my impression that at least 80 to 85 percent of older

men with persistent erection difficulties have some underlying physical problem contributing to their impotence. Often, though, there is a combination of physical and emotional factors, with the physical problems causing initial difficulty and anxiety worsening the problem. I'll discuss ways of telling the physical and emotional factors apart in chapter 24.

# 10

# A Guide for the Older Woman to Using Oral Sex

Although we have frequently mentioned oral lovemaking in the previous two chapters, I am all too aware that many older women are still not comfortable with it. But it is such an effective method for encouraging good erections and maintaining mutual enjoyment that I am devoting this entire chapter to exploring it. You may very well find that greater knowledge will allow you to have increased confidence and, ultimately, success and pleasure in this important technique.

## HE MAY NEED THE EXTRA STIMULATION

As I've stressed, an older man needs more direct stimulation in order to get good erections. Oral stimulation is a very effective way to help. It's also a tender and intimate way to show your caring.

In my treatment of sexual dysfunction, couples often come to me because the man is no longer getting spontaneous erections. This difficulty usually occurs sometime in the

man's forties or fifties, when he starts needing more direct
stimulation to get hard. Embarrassed by his lack of spontaneous erections, he may even start avoiding sex. His partner, while unhappy about the lack of physical contact, may
have rejected the idea of using mouth caresses to help.

They both may miss out by this refusal. She misses a
chance to help her partner and to show her love and affection in a tender and pleasurable way. He fails to get a delightful form of stimulation that might assist him to have
better and more frequent erections. And they both may lose
the chance to continue to enjoy making love and to have
intercourse in a happy and mutually regarding way.

## IT MAY BE DIFFICULT TO TALK ABOUT

Young couples now take oral petting for granted as a natural
part of their lovemaking. A recent study of sexual practices
shows that oral sex is as common as sexual intercourse in the
lovemaking of young adults. On the other hand, many men
and women over forty have lots of inhibitions and taboos
about it.

If you've never used fellatio (stimulating your partner's
penis with your mouth), you may wonder what your partner
would think if you tried it. Many older couples find that it's
difficult to talk about. The man hesitates to ask for it because
he's afraid his partner might be offended. The woman fears
that if she initiates it her partner will be shocked. So neither
of them brings it up.

And so, many women over forty who have tried fellatio
have most probably used it hesitantly. Caroline R., a fifty-
five-year-old woman, told me that she really wanted to help
her husband but didn't know how to use oral sex. "I'm not
sure what Bill would like, or how much pressure to use. I'm
afraid of hurting him with my teeth or just doing it wrong.
I want both of us to enjoy it, but I guess I just don't know
how to begin."

As a woman over forty, you were probably raised with many inhibitions about your own genitals, much less a man's. You may have been raised with the idea that your genital area was dirty and shouldn't even be touched. This kind of indoctrination can make you feel very squeamish about oral lovemaking.

## SKIN IS SKIN AND CLEAN IS CLEAN!

With regard to the issue of cleanliness of the penis and the scrotum, it's most important to realize that skin is just skin. The skin on your partner's penis is no different from the skin on his arm or elbow. If it's clean, it's clean.

It may be reassuring to hear that your mouth has immeasurably more bacteria than the skin on a freshly washed penis. If sterility is your concern, it would make far more sense to give up kissing than fellatio.

You've probably heard a lot of vulgar names for oral sex, but you've probably heard an even greater number of vulgar names for sexual intercourse. So don't let the vocabulary put you off oral lovemaking unless you're prepared to give up intercourse, too.

## IT CAN BE ENJOYABLE FOR YOU, TOO

Although you may be apprehensive about oral lovemaking, it may help you to know that many women find it very enjoyable and exciting for themselves, and not just for their partner.

Think of your partner's penis as your own private plaything. Enjoy its texture and feel, as well as your ability to make it grow. Think of it as a sign of your power that with your tongue and lips *you* can make this soft, small penis grow to be big, full, and firm. You'll find that you will come to enjoy the feel of the penis in your mouth, just as your partner enjoys the feel of your nipple and breast in his. Your mouth, after all, is a very erogenous organ.

## HOW SHOULD I BEGIN?

If using your mouth to stimulate your partner's penis is relatively new to you, you may wonder how to begin. Let me suggest a plan drawn from some of my patients' experiences.

You can reassure yourself about cleanliness beforehand by showering together and washing your partner's penis with soap and water. Remember: when it's washed, it's clean. Showering together has another advantage, as it can also be fun for both of you.

Then start by having your partner lie on his back and gently kiss him along his stomach and legs while you caress his penis with your hands. Then brush your lips along the shaft of his penis with very light kisses at first. This will help you to get accustomed to the feel of it and to reassure yourself that it won't bite.

Now, slowly and gently slide your tongue up and down the underside of the shaft of his penis. As you feel more confident, you can use your tongue to make short licks across the shaft as well as up and down it. The underside of the shaft and the ridge around the head of the penis are especially sensitive.

Some women find that using a flavored lovemaking oil on their partner's penis can be a help in getting over their initial reluctance to oral lovemaking. As an alternative, you may enjoy using some other favorite treats, such as a small amount of honey or chocolate syrup. They may be a little sticky, but if you enjoy the taste enough you won't mind the stickiness at all.

Intersperse licks with gentle kisses. Play your tongue around the ridge near the tip. Flick the little indentation where the ridge meets the underside of the shaft with your tongue. Let the tip of the penis slide into your mouth, and swirl your tongue around it. This will feel very warm, wet, and sensuous to your partner, like having his penis caressed with hot, wet velvet.

Many women who are reluctant at first are amazed to discover how much they enjoy this kind of lovemaking *themselves*. Sixty-year-old Elizabeth W., who had been married for thirty-five years, told me, "I used to think oral sex was something I could never do. I only tried it to help Herb—I felt he really needed me. Now I'm surprised to find out how good it feels to me to have his penis in my mouth. I never would have believed it."

## YOU'LL ENJOY BEING CREATIVE AND PLAYFUL

It's not necessary to try to take the *entire* penis into your mouth. It's much more important to be creative, loving, enthusiastic, and playful. It's fun to be in control of giving your partner such pleasure.

Gradually add slight sucking movements by pulling with your lips as you slide up on the penis. As Elizabeth W. found out, this can be stimulating for you, too. Your lips and tongue are two of your most important sensual organs. That's why people enjoy kissing so much!

Delight in the various sensations of your lips and mouth in contact with your partner's penis and scrotum. The skin of his penis will feel very soft and wrinkly at first. You'll notice the texture changing as you cause his erection to harden. His skin will feel smoother and more velvety to your lips as his penis grows in size. Notice which areas feel best to your lips and which are more exciting to your tongue.

## USE YOUR MOUTH AND HAND
## TOGETHER FOR ADDED PLEASURE

Your partner will be very conscious of the warmth and wetness of your lips and tongue on his penis. If you gently fondle his scrotum at the same time with your hand, it will add a new focus of pleasure.

You can give him even more sensations by initially using your mouth alone, and then adding stimulation with your hand by sliding it up and down the shaft of his penis while your mouth is pulling gently or swirling around its head.

Your partner will find the oral stimulation and the wetness of your lips and tongue to be very exciting. But if you use your lips too lightly he may not get enough sensation. Without the additional stimulation of your hand sliding up and down the shaft of his penis, he may have trouble getting fully hard or climaxing.

It's normal for your jaws to get tired after awhile, especially as it's necessary to keep your mouth fairly wide open to keep your teeth out of the way. Scraping the penis with your teeth can be very distracting, and your partner may well lose his erection. Cushion your teeth by slightly curling your lips over them. If your jaw does get tired, just pause and stimulate your partner with your hand for awhile before resuming your oral caresses.

## "AM I DOING IT RIGHT?"

Women often wonder if they are performing oral sex "correctly." There isn't actually any such thing as *correctly*. It's a question of what feels good to your partner, and the best way to find out is to ask him. As media sex therapist Dr. Ruth Westheimer says, "It is relatively easy to learn how to perform fellatio by practicing on a banana or a lollipop or a

Popsicle. Women who wonder if they are doing it 'right' should ask their partner what feels good to him. . . . It is always a good idea to overcome whatever shyness you feel and discuss with your partner how he or she likes to be pleasured."

## HAVING YOUR PARTNER CLIMAX DURING ORAL SEX IS OPTIONAL

Many men find that climaxing during oral petting is very intense and pleasurable. Some women, in turn, delight in having their partner climax in their mouth, while others don't enjoy this sensation or else enjoy it only occasionally. Those who enjoy it find feeling the contractions and continuing to stimulate the penis with their mouth during climaxing to be intensely arousing. Others enjoy giving their partner pleasure with oral petting but may not want him to climax while they're doing it. It's solely a matter of individual preference.

You can be assured that your partner will have enough warning to let you know when he is about to climax, in case you don't want him to do so while his penis is in your mouth. You will feel the contractions of his penis a second or two before he ejaculates as well. If you want to withdraw your mouth at that time, make sure to *continue stimulation* by sliding your hand up and down his penis. It would be very disconcerting to your partner to have all stimulation stop abruptly, just as his climax is starting.

Semen is a simple liquid containing a number of substances you consume and digest every day: protein, calcium, citric acid, and cholesterol, among others. It usually has very little taste. Some women find the taste of semen pleasant and arousing. Others prefer to follow it with a sweet or pungent substance such as wine or fruit. Certain foods, such as garlic, can impart their taste to a man's semen.

## ORAL LOVEMAKING IS
## LESS PHYSICALLY STRESSFUL

An advantage of fellatio is that it requires much less physical exertion than intercourse does. It can be used in most cases, even if one of you is particularly fatigued or not feeling completely well. This can be especially important if stress to the heart is a concern. It can also be a useful way of making love to your partner if illness, arthritis, or some other problem makes you temporarily unable to enjoy intercourse yourself.

## YOUR PARTNER CAN
## START BY STIMULATING YOU

A nice alternative is to have your male partner begin the lovemaking session by orally stimulating you. *(See chapter 11.)* He can continue until you climax, or else he can stop at an earlier stage, whatever the two of you desire.

You can then use oral caresses to help him to get hard, and from there go on to intercourse. If you don't climax during intercourse but remain stimulated afterward, your partner can bring you to climax at that point.

While it's nice on occasion to have mutual oral lovemaking, it's certainly not necessary or even desirable every time. You and your partner should feel flexible about it, so that, depending on the circumstances of your lovemaking encounter, your partner may orally stimulate you, you may orally stimulate him, or you may both use oral caresses on each other.

Many couples enjoy experimenting with simultaneous oral lovemaking, which is sometimes referred to as "sixty-nine." You can do this with either of you kneeling over the other, with each having his or her head toward the other's genitals. Many people enjoy making love this way, but others find that it can be distracting. It may become difficult to concentrate on what you're doing when you are receiving such intense stimulation.

So oral stimulation can be as varied as intercourse. It can be engaged in just for fun, as a prelude to intercourse, to help your partner get hard, or to bring him to a climax. Use it as an added ingredient in your lovemaking, to be experienced and enjoyed in different ways at different times.

## ORAL LOVEMAKING: AS OLD AS THE HILLS

Oral-genital contact has been a part of sexuality throughout history. Paintings and sculptures from ancient China, Japan, Greece, South America, and Africa show how universal this practice has always been. Yet today we continue to harbor many taboos and inhibitions about it. It's even theoretically illegal in some places.

Actually, using your mouth to give pleasure to your partner is one of the most gentle and intimate ways of expressing sexual love and showing your affection. Values have changed and are continuing to do so to reflect the universality of oral lovemaking. Marriage and sex manuals now devote whole chapters to it, where several decades ago it was hardly mentioned. To quote again from sex therapist Dr. Ruth: "I am not saying everybody is involved with oral sex, but . . . the one thing I can say with assurance to you is that there is nothing abnormal about it."

If you have religious scruples about oral sex, you might consult with your minister, priest, or rabbi. You may be surprised to find that the religious prohibitions you thought existed were misunderstandings on your part.

Needless to say, if either you or your partner have strong objections to this variation of lovemaking, do not feel any pressure to do something you would find disagreeable. If, on the other hand, you simply don't have much experience with oral lovemaking and you have some degree of concern or shyness, be aware that oral lovemaking is not rare and peculiar, but quite common in our society.

Try giving yourself an opportunity to experiment, remembering how exciting those first sexual explorations were. It's fun to have new things to discover, especially now that you're over forty!

# 11

# Enhancing Your Female Partner's Sexual Pleasure

The last three chapters concentrated on ways in which you and your partner can overcome and adapt to the sexual changes that you may experience after forty—most particularly, the slowing of your erection responses and the decreased frequency of your desire for climax. Your over-forty female partner, on the other hand, is unlikely to suffer from the same decreased responses. In fact, she will most likely be quite responsive to anything you can do to increase her enjoyment of lovemaking, to help her to have more satisfying climaxes, and even to please her at times when your own sexual responses may not be as strong as you might like.

As a man over forty, you may never have had the opportunity to actually learn the best ways to stimulate your partner and to bring her to a climax. You probably grew up thinking that whatever was going to happen during sex would happen during standard missionary-position intercourse—and that if your partner didn't climax, then there wasn't much you could do about it.

In fact, in your earliest years of sexual activity, you may not have even known that women were supposed to climax.

One of my patients, Phil E., embarrassedly told me that the first time his wife climaxed he thought that she was having a seizure. While this may be an extreme example, many older men have told me they didn't really have any idea at all how a woman was supposed to respond—or how they could help her—when they were first married.

If you *were* aware that some women climaxed, but if your partner never did, you may have thought that she was "frigid" or had something wrong with her. Your lack of knowledge was due more to the times than lack of interest. You simply had never been taught about the ways that you could help a woman express and enjoy her sexuality. In fact, you probably were discouraged from learning.

Because of the negative attitudes toward sex with which couples now over forty were raised, many of us have never discussed intimate sexual issues with our partners. This lack of communication has made it difficult to learn from each other.

In your grandparents' time, the predominant feeling was that "nice women" weren't supposed to respond sexually. If a woman assumed an active role during lovemaking or even showed sexual arousal, it was likely to be seen as a sure sign that she had loose morals.

The naturalness of female sexual response was eventually recognized, but orgasm during intercourse—and during intercourse only—was still felt to be the only normal way for a woman to climax until the scientific studies of Kinsey and Masters and Johnson appeared in the 1950s and '60s. Before their conclusions were published, a woman who climaxed from clitoral stimulation was considered to be sexually immature. With these studies of actual sexual response, it became clear that *most* women climax primarily and most readily with direct clitoral stimulation, rather than during intercourse. Reports indicated that these women find that vaginal intercourse feels close, satisfying, and arousing, that they enjoy the feeling of having their partner's penis inside them, but that it's not the same kind of feeling that builds to climax for them. They simply require more direct oral or manual stimulation of their clitoris in order to climax. There's nothing wrong with them; it's just the way women's bodies are built and the way their sexual responses naturally are.

## AN ERECTION ISN'T ALWAYS REQUIRED TO SATISFY YOUR PARTNER

The advantage for you as an older man in the way that women climax is that it isn't necessary for you to have an erection every time you want to make love or every time you want to satisfy a woman.

Fred P., one of my patients in his late fifties, told me how pressured he felt to perform sexually if his wife felt like making love but he wasn't up to it. "I know there are times when she really expects us to make love but I'm preoccupied and pooped and don't know if I can get it up—so I try to avoid the whole situation."

Many other men over forty have felt like this at times. When you do, it's important to realize that there are other ways you can satisfy your partner, please her greatly, and enjoy yourself sexually without having to get an erection.

Most older men have had some experience with helping a partner to climax by hand stimulation. However, sometimes either the man or his partner may be self-conscious about manual stimulation, worrying that it's abnormal and that the only "normal" sex is intercourse.

On the contrary, as we have already pointed out, clitoral stimulation is the natural way for most women to climax. Almost all women, for example, stimulate their clitoris when masturbating, while only 5 to 10 percent also insert an object in their vagina. It's clear that women, who are the best judges of what feels good to themselves, find clitoral stimulation to be what produces orgasm for them.

# ORAL LOVEMAKING:
# AN EXCITING ALTERNATIVE

In addition to manual stimulation, which you're probably already familiar with, you both may very much enjoy the variation of using your mouth to stimulate her genital area. This practice, called *cunnilingus,* most women find to be *extremely* pleasurable as well as warm, loving, and intimate. It also provides something that couples who've been together for many years need very much in their lovemaking—variety.

The soft caressing of the clitoris and vaginal lips is very sexually stimulating for women of all ages, and most women climax more readily with cunnilingus than with intercourse. In fact, many women who cannot climax with intercourse at all do so readily with oral stimulation.

Using cunnilingus can relieve a lot of pressure to perform and to get an erection when you just aren't able. Once you've helped your partner to climax with oral stimulation, you can feel confident that she feels both sexually satisfied and secure that you care for her, and she will most likely be content to wait for intercourse until another time when you are ready. Moreover, this is an alternate lovemaking technique that you will greatly enjoy yourself—it's not only sensuous and pleasurable, it can make you proud of your ability to give your partner satisfaction and to help her climax.

Many men in our age group have had little experience with giving oral stimulation, and some of us inevitably have leftover inhibitions about it and are just not comfortable doing it with our wives or partners.

Conversely, most younger people in our society take oral stimulation for granted as a familiar accompaniment to making love and a way of expressing love for their partners. In fact, the 1984 Consumers Union Report, *Love, Sex, and Aging,* found that of the 4000 men and women *over fifty* whom they investigated, half had tried cunnilingus—and the vast majority of both men and women who had tried it had liked it. It certainly might be worthwhile investigating it yourself if you haven't already done so, if only to discover whether you and your own partner would also enjoy it.

## HOW WILL MY PARTNER REACT?

If you haven't used oral stimulation before, your partner might certainly be a little hesitant at first, but she will undoubtedly enjoy it once you begin. Most women achieve a high level of excitation with cunnilingus, and the gentleness and softness of having her clitoris and vaginal lips kissed, licked, and lightly pulled by your lips can help produce an intense orgasm.

It's possible that your partner would like to try cunnilingus but has been afraid to ask about it. She may be reluctant to seem too forward, or she might assume that it would not be appealing to you. Remember that many women over forty have been raised to feel that mouth-genital contact is dirty and forbidden. They have been admonished to not even look at their genitals or touch them. Therefore, they are often surprised to learn that men usually enjoy the intimacy of cunnilingus and, rather than being repelled, find it quite exciting.

In order to introduce oral lovemaking to your partner, you might try discussing it first. On the other hand, it might be best to embark on it in the heat of the moment, to avoid the possible embarrassment or apprehension a self-conscious discussion beforehand might inspire. Your instincts in this matter will be your best guide.

It's probably optimal to pick a time when your partner has just bathed, so she won't be worried about cleanliness or body odor. Bathing or showering together and washing each other just before lovemaking is also a sensual way to establish a mood. Using a fragrant massage or lovemaking oil may also help set her mind at ease.

Your partner's vaginal fluid will probably have no more taste than the taste of saliva when you're kissing. In some cases, there may be a sexy, arousing odor. Any unusual, unpleasant odor that can't be eliminated by bathing would indicate a problem and a visit to her gynecologist would then be in order to see if the cause can be identified and eliminated.

If you are concerned about the sanitary aspects of cunnilingus, keep in mind that unless your partner has a vaginal infection, there are probably many more bacteria and other germs in your mouth than there are in her vagina.

***How to begin.*** As you start mutually caressing and are both becoming sexually excited, use your mouth to kiss and lick her along her thighs and abdomen. These are sensitive areas, and they will also help her get used to having your mouth near her genitals. Then gradually brush your lips through her pubic hair, while you use your hand to stimulate her clitoris.

Your partner may respond with movements or sounds to indicate that she's enjoying what you're doing. If you're not sure, continue to kiss and lick her inner thighs, the crease of her thigh, and her pubic hair in a teasing way. One older woman told me smilingly that she had been apprehensive about her husband trying cunnilingus until she saw how much fun he was having rubbing his nose in her pubic hair. "Then," she said, "I just laughed and relaxed."

If you can tell that she is accepting and enjoying your lovemaking, spread your partner's legs apart and continue using your mouth to stimulate her genitals. This will probably be easiest to do if you lie between her legs while she is on her back with her knees spread apart and bent. You may also want to experiment with other positions, such as positioning yourself alongside her with your knees at the level of her head so she can touch your genitals while you're using your mouth to caress her.

With your partner's legs spread, you'll notice that between the heavier folds of skin that make up the outer lips of her vulva there are two inner flaps, called the minor or inner lips. The vaginal opening is between these inner lips. Where they come together at the top there is a small nubbin of soft tissue, about half the size of the last joint on your pinkie. This is her clitoris. It's the most sensitive sexual area for most women, and it usually enlarges and becomes somewhat erect when a woman is sexually excited.

Other especially sensitive sexual areas will be the inside of her vaginal lips and the area right around the opening of her vagina. Deep inside her vagina there aren't as many nerve endings. The inside of the vagina is therefore less sensitive, except for a particular area of sensitivity called the G-spot, which we will describe in the next chapter.

Spread your partner's inner lips with your fingers and let your tongue run softly up and down the length of them. Then gradually move up her vaginal lips, using stroking, swirling, and licking movements around her clitoris. Some women enjoy stimulation directly on the clitoris, while others find it's too sensitive and prefer circular movements around it. Gentle sucking movements can also be very arousing. There's no rule of thumb here; ask your partner what feels best to her. She may be embarrassed or too shy to tell you what she likes if you don't ask.

If your partner has never experienced oral stimulation before, she may be a little apprehensive and stiff at first, wondering whether you are enjoying it. Reassure her and try to get her to relax and concentrate on the sensations you're creating for her. Tell her to think about what your tongue feels like and to concentrate on the warmth, smoothness, and liquidness of the sensations that she's getting, instead of worrying about you.

While you're stimulating her clitoris with your tongue, you can also stimulate the opening of her vagina with your fingertip, or even fully insert your fingers.

*Will she climax?* Don't expect your partner to climax the first time you try oral stimulation. She may not be able to relax enough, or she may feel too self-conscious.

On the other hand, she may be surprised to climax again and again. An advantage of oral lovemaking is that you can keep the stimulation up indefinitely, until either of you gets tired. And even if she does climax, you can keep licking her clitoris so that she can continue to have orgasms —or else let her rest briefly in between two or more distinct climaxes. Some women find that their clitoris gets too sensitive immediately after one climax to allow them to proceed immediately to another.

Talk with your partner afterward about what it felt like to her. It may be a little difficult for her to sort through her feelings upon experiencing a type of lovemaking that she may have once thought of as shocking or improper. It may actually be disconcerting to her to discover that it felt exciting and it may be difficult to initially acknowledge, even to herself, that she really enjoyed it.

If either of you has reservations after this first experience, don't be discouraged. Give yourselves a chance to become more accustomed to cunnilingus and more comfortable with your own enjoyment of it. Of course, never insist that your partner do anything in lovemaking that she's completely opposed to.

We should mention here that you will undoubtedly enjoy performing oral stimulation yourself. After all, your tongue and lips are among your most erotic organs, and your partner's wetness and softness will feel very pleasant and sensual to them. You will also be excited by her excitement, proud of your ability to express your love in such a warm, intimate way, and of your ability to give your partner such intense feelings of pleasure.

# 12

# More Ways to Please Your Woman Sexually

It's been mentioned that the primary focus of sexual sensitivity for your partner is the area around her clitoris and her inner vaginal lips. But there is another area inside her vagina that may be very sensitive as well: the G-spot, or Graffenberg spot, after the gynecologist who first described it in the 1950s.

Your partner's G-spot is located on the upper wall of her vagina when she's lying on her back. It's about an inch and a half inside her vaginal opening and is approximately the size of a quarter. It tends to feel rough, like tightly packed goosebumps, and swells when it's stimulated.

Women vary a great deal in their degree of sensitivity to G-spot stimulation. If your partner is responsive to this kind of stimulation, you are in a position to give her an incredible amount of sexual pleasure.

## HOW TO STIMULATE
## YOUR PARTNER'S G-SPOT

Whenever trying out a new sexual technique, it's best to do it when the two of you are at leisure to make love and won't be disturbed. Some women get a feeling of needing to urinate when their G-spot is first stimulated, so it might be a good idea for your partner to empty her bladder completely before you begin.

Start by giving your partner a soft back massage to help her relax. Then gradually extend your caresses over her buttocks. Gently caress the back of her legs and slide your hand between them. With her legs spread, apply a little warmed lovemaking oil or other sexual lubricant to her genital area and vaginal opening, and caress her clitoris gently. With your palm down, next gently insert one or two fingers into her vagina. Try stimulating the front wall of her vagina, about three-quarters of an inch past the border of her pubic bone in front. This will be about an inch and a half to two inches inside. Since she's lying on her stomach, you'll be pressing *down,* as if you were pressing toward her belly button.

Slide your fingers forward and back or side to side, and have your partner tell you when you've hit the sensitive place. As I mentioned above, it will probably feel rough, like goosebumps, to you. You may find that it becomes spongy, firm, and swells in size as you continue to stimulate it, much like the erectile tissue in your penis.

Now that you've found the G-spot, kneel between your partner's legs and caress the spot with the fingers of one hand while simultaneously using the thumb of the other to gently stimulate her clitoris. She may be able to climax in this position, or you have the alternative of continuing in a different position.

If your partner turns over onto her back, you can stimulate her G-spot most easily if you lie between her legs. Try inserting two fingers, one above the other, into her vagina and press upward with the tips of your fingers. Move your fingers front to back and side to side. Also, try brushing your thumb or your tongue softly over her clitoris at the same time. Oral stimulation of your partner's clitoris while your fingers are stimulating her G-spot internally can be a very exciting combination of sensations for her. Have her tell you what feels best.

Some women say that their climax has a different feel to it when it comes as a result of G-spot stimulation as opposed to exclusive clitoral stimulation, that it's deeper, more internal. Indeed, if your partner climaxes from G-spot stimulation, you may feel her pushing down against the tips of your fingers inside her vagina, instead of, or in addition to, her muscles squeezing around her vaginal opening, which you usually feel when she climaxes from clitoral stimulation alone.

## TRYING G-SPOT STIMULATION DURING INTERCOURSE

Once you and your partner have located her G-spot, try stimulating it during intercourse. It may be difficult for your penis to make contact with your partner's G-spot in the standard missionary position with her lying on her back, so take this opportunity to experiment with other positions.

One that seems to work very well is the "female superior" position, in which you lie on your back and your female partner kneels over you, facing you. In this position she can probably move her body so that your penis, which is angled forward, can press against her G-spot. Another often successful position is "rear entry," with your penis entering her vagina from behind.

For some women, lying on their back with their legs all the way up on their partner's shoulders enables his penis to contact this most sensitive spot. It sounds acrobatic, but most women don't find it too difficult at all.

Remember that there are *many* different ways to enjoy sex and that there isn't any best or "normal" way. There is individual variation among women, and the G-spot is more sensitive for some than for others. Some women just don't respond strongly to this kind of stimulation, so it's important not to get too involved in trying for a particular type or intensity of sexual response and considering it the only desirable one.

Let the sensitive spot inside your partner's vagina be an additional toy that the two of you can play with. It can become a way of varying your sexual repertoire that you can enjoy together indefinitely.

## HELPING YOUR PARTNER HAVE MORE THAN ONE CLIMAX

You and your partner have probably heard of multiple climaxes for women but may have never really tried to actually achieve them. If she usually has a single clear-cut orgasm, she may never have attempted to climax again after it. If the two of you experiment together, however, you may find that a woman's capacity for more than one climax can add another interesting variation to your lovemaking.

If you are trying to help your partner have multiple climaxes for the first time, the easiest way to begin is for you to stimulate her orally while lying between her legs. Then, while you're licking her clitoris, insert two of your fingers in her vagina to also gently stimulate her G-spot, as we have just described.

You're probably used to ceasing stimulation when your partner reaches her first major climax. This time, keep her clitoris pressed against your lips as she is climaxing and continue to gently stimulate it with your tongue. You may both be surprised to find that she climaxes a second time, and perhaps even a third or fourth, a few seconds apart. Each climax will be a separate peak, without the relaxation that usually occurs after her first climax. She may get tired or too sensitive to continue after several orgasms, but on another occasion she may be curious to see just how many times she can actually climax in a row.

One warning: Sometimes a woman's clitoris becomes exquisitely sensitive immediately after climaxing, so much so that she can't stand to have it touched. If this happens, you can still prolong her excitement by continuing to stimulate her G-spot internally with your fingers while you withdraw your lips from her clitoris. Then, after fifteen or twenty seconds, you can return to extremely gentle clitoral stimulation with your tongue, and gradually build the intensity to help her to climax again.

Don't worry if your partner doesn't climax a second time even with this additional stimulation. The intensity of her first climax may have been so strong that she simply doesn't need additional climaxes.

## A VIBRATOR CAN BE
## A WELCOME ADDITION

Men and women over forty often have little experience with sexual vibrators, which became popular as sexual toys long after most of our sexual training was completed. But vibrators, along with the other sexual suggestions in this book, can be worthy electives in your postforty sexual education.

The vibrator/massager actually provides something new and different. Its rapid vibration applied to sexually sensitive areas provides a stimulation more intense than any that can be provided by simple movement of hand or tongue. Using a vibrator can help you give your female partner a new kind of intense sexual stimulation, as well as providing variety and spice to your lovemaking. You can also be confident that at those times when you're unsure of your erection ability, you can provide pleasure for your partner in an interesting and different way.

There are three basic types of vibrators, all of which are hand held. The first two operate on electrical current and must be plugged into an outlet. The third is usually battery operated.

The first type, sometimes called a Swedish massager, is strapped to the back of your hand so that your fingers and palm pulsate with it. It provides a vibrating sensation through your hand to whatever part of your partner's body you touch. Some people find the sensation to be quite pleasurable, while others find that the vibrator numbs their hand after a while and becomes uncomfortable.

The second type of vibrator is held in your hand rather than strapped to it. It looks something like a compact kitchen mixer. Indeed, some of these vibrator/massagers are made by companies that also make kitchen blenders, such as Oster. This model comes with various small attachments, including cup and disc pieces you can use to stimulate various parts of your own or your partner's body. Women often enjoy having their clitoral area stimulated with a cup-shaped attachment or an attachment with a central ball. Men may enjoy the cup shape over the tip of their penis.

The third type of vibrator is usually battery operated. It's cylindrical and tapered and shaped approximately like a penis. Most often used to stimulate the clitoral area, it sometimes is also inserted into the vagina. Although most women climax primarily with clitoral stimulation, many report that they enjoy the feeling of having the vibrator in their vagina to squeeze on while they're climaxing.

Vibrators are sold in drugstores, department stores, medical supply stores, and by mail. They are often sold as foot, hand, or back massagers, and some buyers actually use them for this purpose.

A caveat concerning battery-operated models: They sometimes turn out to be flimsy in construction, so it's best to make any purchase through a reputable source. It's also important to *always* make sure your vibrator is clean before use.

Following are some suggestions for stimulating your partner with the cylindrical, tapered, penis-shaped vibrator. You can adapt these suggestions to the other two types equally effectively in slightly different ways.

If your partner is lying on her stomach, begin by using the vibrator to give her a relaxing back massage. Then spread your partner's legs gently with your hand and apply a small amount of lovemaking oil or other lubricant to her vaginal area and clitoris. Lubricate the vibrator, as well.

It's pleasurable at all stages to combine vibrator stimulation with your own caresses, using your hands, mouth, and penis. While you slide the vibrator up and down your partner's thighs and approach her vulva in a teasing fashion, gently caress her back and buttocks with your other hand. Then run the length of the vibrator gently down the crease of her buttocks. If the vibrator and her vaginal area are both well lubricated, the vibrator will slip almost effortlessly between her vaginal lips. One of my patients told me that the first time she felt a vibrator in her vaginal area she couldn't believe how intense the sensation was.

Continue to hold the vibrator with one hand while you slide your other hand toward it along her inner thighs. Then run your fingers along her vulval lips and gently caress her clitoris, while the vibrator rests against your fingers. It will feel to her as if your fingers, too, are vibrating, and this will be very stimulating. Ask her at all stages to tell you what feels comfortable, and what degree of pressure she enjoys.

Feel with your fingertip for the opening of her vagina. Then very gradually insert the tip of the vibrator. Slowly, and very gently, continue to slide the vibrator in as you would your penis. Remember, your partner must tell you if it's uncomfortable in any way.

With the vibrator inserted, the stimulation will become even more intense to her. You can add to it by gently sliding the vibrator back out about an inch and then in again in gentle thrusts. If your partner enjoys that, you can add to her sensation by gently moving the vibrator from side to side—

especially if you simultaneously stimulate her clitoris with your free hand. If you have previously located her G-spot, try to stimulate it with the tip of the vibrator. Don't be surprised if she climaxes at this time.

Now let your partner turn over on her back. Slide the vibrator gently up and down her abdomen and around her pubic area. Gently caress one of her breasts with your hand or tongue while you gradually slide the vibrator down past your partner's abdomen and slip it between her legs. Gently slide it forward and back against her vaginal lips while you lick her nipples or caress them with your fingers. She'll enjoy the combination of feelings.

Touch the area around her clitoris softly with the tip of the vibrator, while sliding the fingers of your other hand into her vagina. If you press the vibrator against that hand, your fingers inside her vagina will vibrate, and your partner will receive an interesting and wildly arousing variety of sensations.

Then slide the vibrator gradually into her vaginal opening. Withdraw it an inch or so and gently slide it back in with a soft, thrusting movement. Your partner can have the most exquisite arousal if you manually stimulate her clitoris or lick it at the same time.

Proceed to intercourse at this point, if you wish. Certain positions will even enable you to continue to use the vibrator to stimulate your partner's clitoris while you're inside her. Have her lie on her side, for example, with her back toward you, while you lie on your side behind her. Then come into her vagina from behind. You can easily reach across her abdomen and stimulate her clitoris with the vibrator while your penis is inside her. Use your imagination to devise other ways. Your partner will have the extraordinary feeling of your penis inside her while her clitoris is simultaneously receiving this intense stimulation from the vibrator, and your penis will also feel the vibration through her vaginal walls.

When used in this way, a vibrator can add dimension

and variety to your lovemaking. Many people, however, feel that while the physical sensation produced by the vibrator is intense, there is also a loss of intimacy, resulting in sex that is less emotionally satisfying than that which comes from direct hand-to-body or mouth-to-body contact.

It's also *extremely* important not to use the vibrator too frequently. If your partner uses a vibrator regularly in order to climax, she may become insensitive to other forms of stimulation. The vibrator stimulation is so intense that it's hard for a finger or tongue to compete with it. She can then become dependent on the vibrator in order to climax and may no longer respond to manual or oral stimulation—or even to intercourse—as intensely as she did before. It's therefore wise to keep a vibrator as an *occasional* plaything only, in which case it will be an interesting variation in your lovemaking.

## AN IMPORTANT REVIEW
## ABOUT YOUR PARTNER'S CLIMAXES

There are important points I'd like to make about a woman's sexual responses.

*You partner doesn't need to climax during intercourse.* For most women, intercourse is simply not the best way of producing the stimulation required for orgasm. Although they enjoy the intimacy of intercourse, it just doesn't provide the direct stimulation that enables them to climax.

I have often come across women in my practice who were very sexually responsive, easily aroused, desirous of sex, and who climaxed easily with oral or manual stimulation of the clitoris, but who complained that they were "frigid." It would turn out that they defined themselves as frigid because they didn't climax during intercourse. We now know that such women are normal and sexually responsive, and that most women respond the same way:

they climax more readily, or even *exclusively,* with direct clitoral stimulation.

**Your partner doesn't need to climax at the same time you do.** Another myth that can interfere with your sexual pleasure is the idea that simultaneous orgasms are the best and most satisfying. Some women may indeed prefer this, but it's not a standard that everybody desires or must try to achieve. In fact, many couples feel that it's more pleasurable to climax one at a time, so that each can concentrate while climaxing and the other can have the enjoyment of watching as well. Remember that a woman can climax before, during, or after intercourse—or at all three times, if she likes.

**Your partner doesn't have to have multiple orgasms.** Earlier in this chapter we described how you may be able to help your partner have multiple climaxes. But also remember that there isn't anything wrong with her if she doesn't. Many women experience an extremely satisfying single orgasm, totally complete in itself. Other women vary, sometimes climaxing singly, other times multiply. Neither experience is any better, more sexual, or more successful than the other.

**Your partner doesn't need to climax every time you make love.** There may be times when your partner just doesn't feel the need to climax in a particular lovemaking episode. It may be because she is tired, not feeling quite right, or just feeling less responsive for no particular reason. Leave yourselves open to enjoy whatever happens in your lovemaking without pushing yourselves to meet standards of performance. There may be times when *you* may not have the need to climax but she may have an orgasm, or vice versa. As long as each of you is enjoying the lovemaking and neither of you is feeling taken advantage of, either of these options is perfectly all right. It's only a problem if one or the other of you is *consistently* unable to climax.

# 13

# Prolonging Your Lovemaking for Hours

Men over forty have the advantage of not needing to climax every time they make love. This gives them considerably more flexibility in their sexual relations than they had when they were younger. Now that you're over forty, you can use this flexibility to build your sexual tension or to extend your lovemaking over an entire day or even a weekend.

In this chapter I'll describe how slow, unpressured lovemaking can allow you to be sexually stimulated and intermittently erect all day long—instead of having a disappointing and embarrassing loss of sexual desire and ability after an initial sexual encounter.

You will also learn other ways to turn your ability to enjoy sex without climaxing into an advantage, and how you can use brief lovemaking as an "appetizer" when you're short on time—in anticipation of more extensive love-play later on.

## PROLONGING YOUR
## LOVEMAKING FOR SPECIAL OCCASIONS

You and your partner may be planning a romantic day of lovemaking to celebrate an anniversary, a weekend in the country, or just a rainy Sunday. As a man over forty, however, you may be concerned that after you've made love once, it may take you quite a while until you feel like making love a second time—and longer still until you can get another erection. You'll be glad to know how easy it can be to get around this problem and enjoy doing it.

You can probably remember times when you started out feeling that you wanted to make love all day but found that once you climaxed the first time your sexual drive and interest disappeared. You and your partner may have felt disappointed at having your romantic day cut short, and you may have felt somewhat foolish and embarrassed.

There is an easy way to avoid this. The fall-off in sexual drive doesn't come from *making love,* it comes from *climaxing.* Now that you're older, it will take longer than it did ten, twenty, or thirty years ago to feel like lovemaking again after you've had a climax.

But there is a good-news side to this, too. You can take advantage of another of the changes of aging—your increased ability to enjoy sex without ejaculating—to prolong your lovemaking in a delightful way and to increase your sexual tension at the same time. In many cases, you really *can* make love all day.

## ENJOY SLOW,
## UNPRESSURED LOVEMAKING

Start off with some mutual caressing to help you get hard and your partner lubricated. Because you will be engaged in a lot of sexual activity today, a lovemaking oil will be helpful in keeping the two of you from getting sore. Proceed to intercourse using any position you both enjoy that gives you good control over your ejaculation. Penetrate slowly and leisurely, concentrating on the feeling of your penis inside your partner's vagina.

Take your time kissing and caressing while continuing your slow, luxuriating intercourse. Then, before you get close to climaxing, withdraw but continue caressing. If your erection has gone down, your partner can help you get hard again.

After taking time to relax and caress, return again to slow-paced intercourse. Use a different position if you desire. Again, remember not to push rapidly for climax but rather enjoy the sensual experience. If, for instance, you have inserted your penis into your partner's vagina from behind, the two of you lying on your sides in a spoon position, give her a soft back massage while you continue to gently move your penis in and out. You can stop thrusting for awhile and then restart—or even let your erection go down, withdraw, and return to kissing and caressing.

Most women are able to climax more than once without having their sex drive diminish. Your partner may climax anytime during this first session of lovemaking, or else allow her sexual tension to build along with yours until later in the day.

## YOU MAY FEEL STIMULATED ALL DAY

The two of you can then take a break and go to lunch, take a walk, or enjoy some other activity. You'll discover that since you've had so much sexual stimulation without ejaculation, instead of feeling fully sated, as you would have if you had climaxed, you will continue to enjoy the sensation of being sexually aroused throughout your other activities. You may both continue to have thoughts and fantasies about sex and feel anxious to get back to another lovemaking session in the afternoon.

When you return to continue your celebration, your partner can help you to get erect again, and you can also resume caressing her. The two of you may alternate manual with oral petting to excite each other and have relaxed episodes of intercourse.

After another hour or more of leisurely lovemaking in the afternoon, you can break for another activity and take up lovemaking once more in the evening. Or you can finish your lovemaking by climaxing at any other time.

After holding off from climaxing over a long period of time, you may occasionally find that you are unable to come when you finally want to. If so, don't worry about it. Just wait until the next sexual opportunity and let yourself climax easily the first time.

This kind of prolonged lovemaking without climaxing has wonderful advantages for those occasions when you have all the time in the world. It allows a slow, leisurely, and especially tender sharing.

Prolonged lovemaking isn't always necessary. Many times, sex will be complete in a single episode, and that's perfectly all right. But for those times when you know that there will be many sexual opportunities during a day or weekend, and you would like to make love more than once, prolonged lovemaking without climaxing can greatly increase your pleasure.

## THE APPETIZER:
## WHEN THERE ISN'T TIME FOR MORE

Your advantage of not needing to climax every time can also give you a lot more flexibility on those occasions when you and your partner are both sexually excited and want to make love but you have only a few minutes for lovemaking. You may have to get dressed soon to go out for dinner or to go to work. You may already be dressed. Company may be expected at any moment, or an appointment may have to be kept. It may even be late at night, and you have to arise early in the morning. You may feel like making love but know that you don't have time for full, extended lovemaking.

Let's assume that the two of you have just showered and have company arriving in forty-five minutes. Showering together has gotten you both sexually interested, but you must dress and finish preparing for your guests. You realize that the extended lovemaking session you both want must be postponed until after the company leaves. This is a good time for a little "warm-up."

Ask your partner if she would like to "play" a little before you get dressed. If she's receptive, you can begin mutual caressing. As you caress and stroke each other, you will probably both become aroused. Your partner can help you get fully erect. Some oral stimulation may be especially helpful to you at a time like this—and you can use it as well to help your partner become rapidly lubricated. Applying a sexual lubricant to your penis and to her vagina will also help you achieve an easy entry.

When you are fairly hard and well lubricated, you can slide into your partner for a little sexual appetizer and promise of things to come. *Don't* rush, and *don't* try to climax. Make some nice, gentle thrusts and press yourself fully inside her.

This little appetizer can be as brief as four or five strokes or as long as four or five minutes before you withdraw without climaxing. It's a wonderful way of letting each other know how much you care about each other. And, during dinner, you can both be thinking about how much you'll enjoy "dessert."

You can even try a sexual appetizer when you're both fully dressed, though it will require you to be a little more imaginative and uninhibited.

Let's say that this time you only have *fifteen* minutes until the guests are due to arrive, and you don't have time to get fully undressed and dressed again. On the other hand, you're both feeling sexy and would like a little love-play.

Your partner can open your pants and caress your penis manually or orally to help you get hard. If she is wearing a skirt, put your hand under it and caress her genital area to help her lubricate while she's caressing you. A small amount of lovemaking oil carefully applied so as not to get any on her clothing will be very helpful.

When you're erect and she's lubricated, she can simply slip off her panties or pantyhose and lean over a counter, a bed, or the dining room table. Pull her skirt up over her buttocks from behind and, with you standing behind her, let her guide your penis into her vagina. You will both find it very exciting when you caress her buttocks and genitals with her dress pulled up or her slacks pulled down. If necessary, you both can be fully dressed again in seconds!

Again, just a few strokes or a few minutes of lovemaking in a position like this will leave you both feeling very daring, sexually stimulated, and looking forward to lovemaking later. The experience of brief intercourse without orgasm is a wonderful way of showing your desire for each other when time is limited. You may occasionally have difficulty getting hard because you're worried that the time is short. Trying to get an erection quickly can cause occasional problems for *anyone.* If you do have difficulty, don't be concerned. Just enjoy the fun and warmth of caressing each other sexually, and try again at another time.

## MIDDLE-OF-THE-NIGHT, HALF-ASLEEP PLAY

The ability to make love without needing to climax can be enjoyed at those times when you're just dozing off or when you wake up warm and cuddly in the middle of the night or in the morning. You may both be half-asleep and not up to fully energetic lovemaking, but you may also feel sensuous and a little excited.

Let's say, for example, your partner is tired and you're

giving her a back rub to help her relax. As she starts dozing off, slide one of your massaging hands down between her legs and gradually and gently caress her vulva and help her lubricate without fully waking her. Continue to rub her back with the other hand. Go back and forth for a while, rubbing her back, then returning to her vulva, and adding a little oil so that she will be quite wet. You will likely be partially erect from stimulating her, and then, by gently rubbing your penis against her thigh, you may become fully hard.

Put a little oil on your own penis for lubrication, spread her legs, and slip gently inside her while she continues to lie face down, half-dozing. She need not fully awaken, but it will help if she tilts her pelvis up toward you or if you slip a pillow under her to facilitate penetration.

After thrusting softly for a minute or two, you can then both roll over on your sides, with your penis still inside her vagina from behind. After a few more gentle thrusts, you can both fall asleep with you still inside her, a very tender and romantic way of living out a sexual fantasy.

Another scenario: You awaken in the early-morning hours with an erection. If your partner is sleeping with her back toward you, you can gently stroke her vaginal area from behind to see if she is receptive. If she seems to enjoy what you're doing, lubricate her vaginal area with some oil that you keep by the bedside, making sure to warm the oil briefly in your hand first.

Then gently slip your penis inside her. If you're both three-quarters asleep, you can make just a few thrusting movements and fall asleep again. Your penis will, of course, slip out as your erection goes down, but you will both re-awaken later in the morning feeling terrific and loved. You can finish your lovemaking when you're fully awake, or else save it for evening.

Make sure you let your partner know how much you appreciate her loving cooperation and how wonderful it makes you feel to know that you can initiate love-play at almost any time and to know that in most cases she will be lovingly receptive. Remember that these little nighttime or morning play sessions don't have to go anywhere. You don't have to climax during them. They are just a sign of your love and affection for each other.

## BUILDING SEXUAL TENSION

A final benefit of lovemaking without climaxing is that it can be used to greatly increase your level of sexual tension. If you become sexually aroused two or three times in the course of a day from manual or oral stimulation of your penis, as well as intercourse, and if you continue again the next day with more of the same without climaxing, you may start to feel an increased sense of sexual urgency and desire that you may not have experienced for a long time. You may find yourself thinking more sexually, feeling more sensitivity from your penis, and even becoming aroused and erect more easily. While frequently repeated sexual arousal with a delayed climax may not be practical on a regular basis, it's a real delight on occasion.

# 14

# Simple Exercises to Strengthen Your Sexual Muscles

I'm often asked whether there are exercises that can help improve sexual functioning and sexual response. There are, and they can be used by both men and women to strengthen their sexual muscles and improve their responses. Called Kegel exercises, they can be especially important for older men and women, to prevent the loss of pelvic muscle tone that might otherwise come with aging.

As a woman over forty, you may have noticed that the muscles around your vagina have lost some of their tone and are looser than they used to be, especially if you have had several children. This may give you and your partner less friction and, consequently, less intensity during intercourse. Doing Kegel exercises can help you tighten these muscles yourself without surgery. Moreover, Kegels can improve your vaginal tone and enable you to climax more easily, with more intense orgasms. Your strengthened vaginal muscles will also provide more friction during intercourse and allow you to squeeze your partner's penis more tightly. This may be especially important if his erection is not quite fully firm at first, which is not uncommon for older men.

Some women also feel that doing the sexual exercises can increase their sexual desire. In fact, one forty-year-old patient recently told me, "When I do my Kegel exercises regularly, I feel like having sex all the time." My guess is that doing her exercises actually makes her more conscious of her sexual feelings.

Many men also feel that the Kegel exercises help them sexually. Some of my male patients say the exercises give them more control over premature ejaculation, help them have stronger, more pleasurable orgasms, and help with erection problems.

## HOW A WOMAN CAN STRENGTHEN HER SEXUAL MUSCLES

Your sexual muscle is the pubococcygeus, often called the PC muscle. It surrounds the opening to your vagina and extends from your pubic bone to your tailbone, or coccyx.

For many women the PC muscle loses its tone and tightness with age. If the problem becomes severe, these vaginal muscles can be repaired and tightened surgically. In most cases, however, this isn't necessary. You can perform a simple set of exercises to tighten and tone your PC muscles yourself.

These exercises were developed several decades ago by Dr. Arnold Kegel, who originally used them to help women tighten their vaginas and overcome urinary stress incontinence after childbirth.

The easiest way for a woman to locate her PC muscle is to discover it during urination. While urinating, try stopping and starting the urine flow with your legs spread wide apart. The muscle that you squeeze to stop the flow is your PC muscle. Check by inserting your finger into your vagina and contracting your muscle just the way you did to stop urinating. If you have any muscle tone, you should notice a slight tightening of the vagina around your finger.

When you have a clear idea of what the contractions feel like, allow yourself a few minutes to practice them. While lying comfortably on your bed, tighten and then release the muscle ten times. Gradually increase this from day to day until you are doing fifty contractions each day.

Once you have developed some ease with these exercises, you can do them at any time—while you're driving your car, sitting at your desk, or talking on the telephone, and no one else will ever know what you're doing.

Once you can do fifty contractions fairly easily, you can begin some variations: First, quickly contract or tighten the muscle, then very gradually relax it. Do ten of these variations and add them in as part of your usual fifty per day.

The second series of variations is a fast tightening followed by a fast relaxation. This is a speeded-up version of what you were doing all along. Again, include this variation among the fifty that you are doing daily.

The third variation is to tighten very, very slowly, being aware of how deep in the vagina you can feel the contraction. When you feel your entire pelvic area totally tensed, quickly relax. This may take some practice, so don't become discouraged if you have some difficulty feeling it.

After you've built up your strength so that you can do these exercises easily and when you can feel a definite squeeze on your finger when you contract your muscle, you can drop down to doing only twenty per day. You will have developed good tone and control at this point, so you will just be maintaining your muscle strength. Some women, however, continue to do fifty or more squeezes a day, either because it increases their sexual awareness or because they wish to build their ability to grip their partner's penis during intercourse.

Some women report that they climax more readily as they develop more strength in their PC muscles. Other women find that their enjoyment of their orgasm is greater because their contractions are more intense. As we noted before, strengthening your PC muscle can also increase your

SEX OVER 40

partner's enjoyment, since you can readily squeeze to stimulate his penis during intercourse. He will also be able to feel your more intense contractions during orgasm.

Of equal importance, PC exercises are a significant way for you to continue to maintain and care for your sexual system as you age. Maintaining the PC muscle is not only a daily exercise of your sexual system, it's an investment in sexual enjoyment.

## HOW MEN CAN STRENGTHEN
## THEIR OWN SEXUAL MUSCLES

Men, too, can benefit greatly from doing Kegel exercises. Your penis gets erect not from tightening a muscle but because it fills with blood. There aren't any significant muscles in the penis itself, but the entire base of the penis, which is inside your body, is surrounded by your pelvic muscles. The sexual benefits of strengthening the male PC muscle have not been scientifically proven, but there is accumulating empirical evidence that it helps in a number of ways.

In the first place, strengthening and exercising the pelvic muscles surrounding the base of your penis will help to increase the blood supply to those muscles and to the entire pelvic area, including the penis. This can improve the circulation of blood in the penis and, theoretically, improve erections in that way.

Second, if not exercised, the PC muscle tends to atrophy somewhat with age. Since one of the features of orgasm is the rhythmic contraction of this muscle, its atrophy means decreased sensation from orgasm.

Thus, exercising your PC muscle and strengthening it may give you stronger, more pleasurable orgasms. It may also help you to develop better control over your ejaculation as you become more consciously aware of your sexual response. With practice, men can learn to either firmly contract or consciously relax this muscle, so that they can voluntarily delay the onset of ejaculation.

A number of patients over forty have told me that doing Kegel exercises has also improved their prostate function. In fact, several have said that their bouts with chronic prostatitis, which had previously required frequent or continuous antibiotic therapy, had subsided completely after several months of doing Kegel exercises. Urologists I have checked with don't know of any studies that prove Kegel exercises actually help prostatitis, but since contractions of the PC muscle may help the prostate to drain and may increase blood circulation in the area of the gland, it's certainly possible that these exercises might be beneficial. At any rate, they are something very simple that you can do yourself which might help and won't be of any harm.

You can locate your PC muscle the same way we directed women to locate theirs earlier in the chapter. Try stopping and starting the flow of urine while you're urinating. Or else, pretend that you're trying to hold in a bowel movement. The muscles you squeeze to do this are the pelvic muscles you're looking for.

Once you've located the muscles, try squeezing and releasing them fifteen times twice a day. Gradually increase the number of contractions from day to day, until you're doing fifty at a time.

At this point you can add a variation. Contract your pelvic muscles and hold them for three seconds before you relax. Try to work up to doing fifty of these longer Kegel exercises twice a day. You can alternate a series of these with the regular short Kegels.

It may take a month until you begin to feel sexual benefits from these exercises, but you probably should continue them for at least six weeks to see if they will be helpful for you.

# 15

# Masturbation for Older Men and Women

Older men and women alike may find themselves without sexual partners at times. Divorce, death, or temporary separation might be the reason, or else a spouse may not be willing or able to engage in sex for a variety of reasons, including illness. At times like this, self-stimulation (or masturbation), as a way of dealing with your normal sexual desire, is a common, sensible solution.

Many of us who are over forty received our ideas about masturbation from parents with prejudices left over from the Victorian era. It's difficult now, in retrospect, to imagine how such a safe, harmless practice could arouse such phobias. After all, when you pleasure yourself, no one becomes pregnant, is molested, catches a venereal disease, or is harmed in any way.

## SELF-STIMULATION
## STARTS IN CHILDHOOD

Self-stimulation as a way to give oneself pleasure begins at infancy as soon as children have enough motor coordination to find their genitals. Most children of three, four, or five years of age stimulate themselves sexually, not because they have any idea of what sexual intercourse is, but simply because it feels good.

Almost all adolescent boys and about two-thirds of adolescent girls masturbate. The high frequency of masturbation during adolescence doesn't mean that masturbation is a particularly adolescent activity. It merely reflects the fact that adolescents don't have readily available sexual partners. Masturbation resumes or continues, for most men and women, at other times in their lives when they don't have a regular partner. It doesn't represent sexual immaturity or perversion. It just represents not having someone else to have sex with.

A recent survey of older men and women found that two-thirds of men (and half of women) in their fifties masturbate at various times. Even among men and women *seventy and over,* a third or more continue to masturbate. And the practice isn't limited to unmarried men and women either; many married people aged fifty and over also masturbate at times.

The more education a person has, the more likely he or she is to use masturbation. For instance, college-educated men and women are more likely to masturbate than those with less education. They are more likely to be aware of the foolishness of the myths about masturbation and more likely to feel that sex is a normal and necessary function that should be enjoyed. Thus, if they don't have a partner, they try to enjoy sex without one.

## BENEFITS OF MASTURBATION

If you're over forty, continuing some form of sexual activity is important as a way of keeping your sexual organs and sexual physiology healthy and functioning. If you go for a long time without using your sexual organs, resuming sex may become much more difficult. If, for example, a man has been having regular erections with masturbation, it will be much easier for him to function in a sexual situation than if he had not had any erections for years. Similarly, lack of regular arousal for a long period of time may make it more difficult for a woman to get lubricated and aroused and to accommodate a penis. Masturbation is a good way of keeping sexual function intact during that time when a partner is unavailable.

Some couples additionally include masturbation as an occasional part of their lovemaking together. They find it arousing to watch each other masturbate, and they also learn from their partners' techniques of pleasuring themselves what forms of physical stimulation are especially enjoyable for them.

## INCREASE YOUR
## ENJOYMENT OF MASTURBATION

Masturbation cannot make up for the lack of a sexual partner, and despite the physical benefits, it's natural to have some feelings of being unfulfilled. There are, however, some things that you can do to make masturbation more interesting and pleasurable for yourself.

To start off with, allow yourself plenty of time. Pleasuring yourself isn't something to just rush through and get out of the way. Prepare some atmosphere: candlelight, music perhaps, and ensure privacy by unplugging your telephone.

Fantasy, common for both men and women during masturbation, will enable you to feel more sexual and aroused. You can help yourself fantasize by reading sexually oriented books or watching erotic videotapes.

Lubricants will help to simulate the wetness of sexual intercourse. They also prevent irritation and make masturbation more comfortable and pleasant.

New ways of masturbating will vary your experience, so experiment with new techniques. Try stimulating different areas of your body, such as your nipples, and caressing yourself with different kinds of fabrics, such as silk or velour. If you have privacy, use different rooms of your house, or even the outdoors.

A vibrator can provide variety as well as extra stimulation. A woman can use it on her clitoris or a man on the head of his penis. Some women enjoy the pulsating quality of a stream of water from their shower attachment while they lie in the tub.

Use your imagination so that masturbation can provide you pleasure and sexual relief when your partner is not available and help to keep your sexual mechanism functioning and well.

# PART III

# SEX AND YOUR HEALTH OVER 40

# 16

# Satisfying Sex in Spite of Arthritis and Lower Back Pain

More people in this country are affected by arthritis than by any other disease, and most of these people are over forty.

Unfortunately, if you have arthritis, you know that the stiffness, pain, fatigue, and limitation of motion that too often accompany this illness can unquestionably affect your sexual life, as can lower back pain, which also afflicts many people over forty. This chapter will offer ways that you and your partner can adapt and adjust to these problems so you can continue to enjoy a full sex life together.

Arthritis limits physical activity—all kinds of physical activity. If you have arthritis, you may lose the ease and comfort of movement that you once had. Mobility in some of your joints may be lost completely, as may the dexterity of the fine movements of your hands. Unfortunately, in addition to limiting other physical activity, the discomfort of arthritis can markedly limit a person's sexual activity.

I remember fifty-year-old Rebecca W. telling me, "Sometimes the pain was excruciating when I tried to spread my legs for intercourse. It didn't happen every time, but after a while I became afraid to try. It's hard to feel sexy when you're waiting for a stab of pain." I couldn't argue with that, but I was able to show her how to enjoy sex again —in ways I'll discuss later in this chapter.

The pain of arthritis can influence your sexual life in two ways. First, it may have a *direct effect:* It may make it difficult to reach orgasm if, for instance, the position that you're using for lovemaking causes your hip to hurt, or if you are afraid that pain may start. Second, there may be an *indirect effect:* Chronic pain anywhere in your body can decrease your sexual drive and distract you during lovemaking, even if the joint involved has nothing to do with the lovemaking itself.

It's not only the pain and stiffness of arthritis that can limit your sexual activity. You may also inhibit yourself due to lack of confidence about your physical appearance, since arthritis may cause swelling and deformity in some of your joints.

The role you take in sex can also influence your feelings. Men who are used to being the more active partner in lovemaking may feel that they're giving up their masculine role if they have to limit their movements and let their partners take over the more active role.

## YOUR PARTNER MAY HOLD BACK TOO

If your partner knows that you have pain and discomfort during sex, he or she may avoid suggesting lovemaking altogether rather than cause you discomfort and may even feel guilty and selfish about suggesting it knowing it may be uncomfortable for you.

## THE MANY BENEFITS
## TO STAYING SEXUALLY ACTIVE

It's extraordinarily important to keep a positive attitude toward lovemaking and to stay as sexually active as you can, even with arthritis. Successful lovemaking will improve your image of yourself and increase your self-esteem. It's a wonderfully effective way to restore your self-confidence in your physical self and reinforce your feeling of masculinity or femininity.

Sex may relieve pain too. Some people experience pain relief for up to six to eight hours after sexual relations. It is thought that this may be due to the body's release of *endorphins,* its internal pain relievers, during sexual stimulation and especially during orgasm.

You and your partner can take a number of basic steps to help you overcome some of the sexual problems caused by arthritis. The steps may be simple, but they can be very important. Some may seem unromantic and unspontaneous to you, but your lovemaking will probably be more enjoyable if it's planned but pain-free than it will be if it's spontaneous but uncomfortable.

## STEP 1: WORK WITH YOUR
## PARTNER ON HOW YOU BOTH CAN
## ADAPT TO YOUR PHYSICAL LIMITATIONS

Let your partner know what touches are uncomfortable or painful. Guide your partner's hand with yours to show him or her which tender areas need to be avoided. Also show your partner how he or she can stimulate you without causing you pain.

You may not have talked about things like this in specific ways before, but doing so now can be crucial. Your partner will have less worry about causing you pain while caressing you if you've explained your sensitive areas in

advance. And you will be better able to relax and enjoy
lovemaking as well if you know that he or she is aware of
your particularly painful points and will try to avoid them.

## STEP 2: DEVELOP A CLEAR
## SIGNAL TO COMMUNICATE DISCOMFORT

Developing a clear signal in advance will allow you to let
your partner know quickly and easily if lovemaking becomes uncomfortable for you. A tap on the shoulder, for
instance, may be much less disruptive to the lovemaking
mood than saying "Ouch!" or "Stop!"

## STEP 3: CHOOSE THE
## BEST TIME OF DAY FOR YOU

Different types of arthritis have different patterns of discomfort throughout the day. If, for example, you have rheu-
matoid arthritis, you may feel particularly stiff in the morning and better later in the day. If, on the other hand, you
have osteoarthritis, you may feel worse in the evening and
better in the morning. Choose your best time of day for
making love. Try to adapt your lovemaking schedule to your
own body's needs. For instance, if you feel stiff in the morning, but tired in the evening, try to make love in the afternoon whenever possible. Take advantage of the time after
you feel loosened up but before you become fatigued.

## STEP 4: PLAN AROUND
## YOUR MEDICATION SCHEDULE

Some people with arthritis or back pain take pain medication or anti-inflammatory medication on a regular schedule.
If you do, try to plan your lovemaking around it. You proba-

bly know approximately how quickly your medication takes effect, so try for that period when the medication is at peak effectiveness. On the other hand, if your medication sedates you or dulls your sensitivity, you might wish to wait until the sedation passes or to discuss a change in your medication with your physician.

## STEP 5: LOOSEN UP BEFORE LOVEMAKING

If exercise takes some of the stiffness out of your joints, do some loosening up before lovemaking. You and your partner might want to exercise together.

## STEP 6: MOIST HEAT HELPS

Take a warm shower or bath together before lovemaking, or try a bubble bath. Moist heat will help to loosen up your joints and diminish pain, and it can be a sensual experience as well.

If you enjoy applying body lotion to each other after your bath, this too can be a delightful prelude to lovemaking. A gentle body massage can also help you to feel more comfortable and more sensual.

## STEP 7: YOU MAY NEED A SEXUAL LUBRICANT

Some forms of arthritis can be accompanied by a condition called Sjogrens Syndrome, which causes a decrease in secretions throughout your body, including vaginal lubrication. The lack of vaginal lubrication is part of your medical condition. It doesn't mean that you're not responding sexually.

If you should experience a decrease in vaginal lubrication due to your arthritis, a lovemaking oil or other sexual lubricant can make lovemaking much more comfortable.

## STEP 8: TAKE ADVANTAGE
## OF COMFORTABLE POSITIONS

One of the ways that you can adapt your lovemaking to get around the problems of arthritis is to choose comfortable positions for intercourse. These will vary according to your specific needs.

The standard "missionary position," in which the man supports himself over the woman while she lies with her legs spread, can be uncomfortable for a man if he has arm or shoulder problems, and it may be painful or even impossible for a woman with arthritis in her hips.

The accompanying illustrations depict some positions that may be especially comfortable for people with arthritis. Look them over and choose the ones you can adapt to your own individual problems. (Actually, these positions might be worth a try whether or not you have arthritis.)

Pillows placed under your buttocks or knees will help in some positions. Knee pads, which can be purchased in most medical supply houses, can cushion painful joints.

*Figure 16–1* illustrates what I'll call the "spoon position." Both partners lie on their sides with the man behind the woman. The man's penis enters the woman's vagina from behind. If it aids in comfort, the woman can place a pillow between her legs.

This comfortable position doesn't require either partner to support his or her weight on arms or knees. It's especially useful when the woman has hip involvement.

*Figure 16–2.* Here the woman lies on her back with her knees bent over her partner's hips. It's another helpful position if the woman has back trouble or difficulty bending her

Fig. 16.1

Fig. 16.2

Illustrations courtesy of the Arthritis Foundation.

Fig. 16.3

Fig. 16.4

Fig. 16.5

Illustrations courtesy of the Arthritis Foundation.

hips or legs. It allows the partners to see each other and for the man to caress the woman's breasts during intercourse.

*Figure 16–3.* Both of you stand, with the woman leaning forward over a piece of furniture that is at a comfortable enough height for her to lean on for support and balance, while the man enters from behind. A pillow under her arms can provide extra comfort.

*Figure 16–4.* The woman kneels over a piece of low furniture, such as a soft hassock, with her knees resting on a pillow. This position is helpful if she has hip problems, but it may be uncomfortable if her shoulders are affected.

*Figure 16–5.* The man lies on his back while the woman kneels over him. He can use pillows to support his knees if desired. This is an especially good position if the man has hip, knee, or back complications.

## STEP 9: ORAL STIMULATION CAN SUBSTITUTE FOR ARTHRITIC HANDS

Arthritis in your hands may make difficult the kind of fine, gentle movements that you would like to use in caressing your partner. If this is the case, oral stimulation can be a very important substitute.

## STEP 10: GET TREATMENT FOR DEPRESSION

Depression can drain your sexual desire, and it's easy to get depressed when arthritis or back pain greatly interferes with important aspects of your life. If you do become depressed, discuss this problem with your doctor. Psychotherapy can be very important in helping you adjust to the changes in

your life and self-image that can result from arthritis. Antidepressant medications can also help you to feel less depressed very rapidly—and this, of course, can help bring
back your desire for lovemaking.

## STEP 11: USE OTHER MEANS
## OF STIMULATION WHEN YOUR
## ARTHRITIS IS ESPECIALLY BAD

At times when arthritis flares up and becomes particularly
troublesome you may find intercourse too uncomfortable,
but you may still want to continue to enjoy mutual lovemaking for the intimacy it brings.

You and your partner can use manual or oral stimulation at these times to please each other sexually. Even when
you don't feel well enough to enjoy being stimulated yourself, you may still wish to so pleasure and satisfy your
partner. Consider the vibrator as another way to assist either
of you to climax at times when intercourse is impossible. (See
chapter 12 for more information on vibrators.)

## STEP 12: MAINTAIN A POSITIVE
## ATTITUDE TOWARD LOVEMAKING

In many cases it's not the physical problems that impair
lovemaking as much as emotionally giving up. A strong
desire to continue lovemaking can help you find a way
around almost any physical impairment.

Don't feel locked into the positions for intercourse that
you used before you developed arthritis or back trouble.
Work on getting rid of preconceptions and prejudices about
alternate ways of caressing, such as oral lovemaking. You
may have to modify your lovemaking and use different
methods of stimulation than you did before. Discard the
inappropriate guilt feelings that you may have about mak-

ing these changes in your lovemaking pattern. Some positive changes can result from your adversity; your lovemaking may end up more interesting and varied than before.

You may also feel guilty at times, because in having to abstain from intercourse you may fear you're also depriving your partner. If this happens, it's important that the two of you *talk* about it. Remember that you can satisfy your partner by other means, even if you're temporarily unable to have intercourse.

These twelve steps won't make your physical difficulties disappear, but they can help you to keep your sexual life active and enjoyable, allowing you to continue to feel loved and loving—which is extremely important to each and every one of us.

# 17

# Painful Intercourse: It's Not "All in Your Head"

Most women experience occasional episodes of lovemaking in which intercourse is uncomfortable. Sometimes the discomfort subsides quickly, after the first few strokes. At other times, a slight discomfort may last throughout intercourse. This may not even be a problem for you if it doesn't interfere with your enjoyment.

But for many older women, the experience of chronic pain or discomfort during intercourse is a constant frustration. Their doctors often assume that their pain is caused by psychological factors if a physical cause isn't immediately obvious. And then even when a physical problem *is* found, they are likely to be told that their "mild" vaginal infection or "small" scar is insignificant and shouldn't be all that painful. The implication, then, is that since "nothing much" has been found, the problem is mostly mental.

On the contrary, just the opposite is usually true. The psychological problems that arise often result from the frustration of having real and chronic pain during sex, an activity that should be pleasant and enjoyable. Women who have pain with intercourse, a condition known as *dyspareunia,* often *do* develop a negative attitude: "Sex just really hurts," blurted out a patient, after much evasion, "so why should I want it? There's no pleasure in it for me."

If you have repeated episodes of severe pain or discomfort with intercourse, you may develop a complication whereby the muscles around your vaginal opening go into involuntary spasm and clamp shut at the approach of your partner's penis. This is called *vaginismus,* and it can make intercourse impossible.

Vaginismus is an involuntary reflex. It's your body's way of flinching from pain. Sometimes vaginismus continues even when the original cause of the pain, such as an infection, is no longer present. Unfortunately, the vaginismus itself may then continue to make sexual attempts painful.

Although you may be having real pain, psychological factors can affect the way you perceive it. If, for example, you are generally unhappy about your relationship and you're not eager to make love, minor discomforts can become magnified, often without your realizing it.

Even when you are happy with your partner and desire lovemaking, anxiety about repeated pain can certainly create the beginnings of a vicious cycle: if sex has been consistently painful, you're bound to have apprehension about it, and that apprehension in turn can make you more sensitive to pain.

It may, then, be somewhat reassuring to hear that when a woman over forty who has enjoyed intercourse for years develops persistent severe pain on intercourse, there is probably a physical, treatable cause for it.

## TYPES AND CAUSES OF PAINFUL INTERCOURSE

Painful intercourse—dyspareunia—is categorized into two types. *Superficial dyspareunia* refers to pain felt at the opening of the vagina when the penis first penetrates. The pain may continue when the penis has fully entered. It's usually due to a vaginal problem or to vaginismus.

On the other hand, *deep,* or *thrusting, dyspareunia,* does not usually involve any discomfort on initial entry, but a great deal of pain when the penis thrusts against tender areas on the uterus, fallopian tubes, or surrounding structures deep inside the vagina.

*Superficial dyspareunia.* This condition is usually due to vaginitis or to lack of lubrication. In older women who are postmenopausal, it's usually caused by lack of estrogen, which produces *atrophic vaginitis.* This refers to thinning of the vaginal wall, with subsequent loss of the protective folds of the vaginal lining, loss of lubrication, and increased susceptibility to abrasion and infections. As described in chapter 3, atrophic vaginitis can usually be effectively treated by estrogen replacement therapy and/or by locally applied vaginal estrogen creams. If you can't use estrogens, vaginal lubricants and lovemaking oils may be helpful.

Of course, other circumstances can account for insufficient lubrication in a woman of any age. They include lack of arousal, a feeling of being rushed, anxiety for any reason, or fear of recurrence of previous painful intercourse. Even the use of a tampon can cause a temporary dryness, because of its absorption of moisture.

Moreover, postmenopausal women, like women of any age, can develop a variety of common vaginal infections, which are another cause of superficial dyspareunia. The most common are yeast infections (monilia), nonspecific vaginitis due to gardnerella, and trichomonal vaginitis. Some forms of vaginitis aren't apparent on routine gynecological exams, and so it may be necessary to take special vaginal smears, cultures, or other laboratory tests to find them. But once identified, they usually can be easily treated with antibiotics or other appropriate therapy.

Vaginitis can cause vaginal pain or burning, including burning on urination, and can continue for up to twenty-four hours after intercourse. This can certainly be enough to make a woman think twice about sexual relations, and even avoid them if it happens consistently.

Other infections that can cause pain include venereal warts, herpes lesions, and cysts or infections of the Bartholin glands. Venereal warts and herpes are usually sexually transmitted; Bartholin gland infections also may result from sexually transmitted infections.

A final cause of superficial dyspareunia can be sensitive scars, whether from childbirth, episiotomy, or other prior surgery or injury.

*Deep, or thrusting, dyspareunia.* Pain with deep thrusting of the penis is often localized at a specific point or points of tenderness inside the vagina. It can sometimes be avoided by trying different positions for intercourse.

Endometriosis is a common cause of such pain in women who are still menstruating. This condition, which results from growth of uterine tissue in the pelvic area outside the uterus, is never malignant. The uterine tissue responds to hormonal changes, which causes the pain to be most prominent when the woman is premenstrual.

Many women, even without endometriosis, find that around the time of their period their uterus is simply more tender and sensitive to deep thrusting during intercourse.

Other common causes for deep dyspareunia in premenopausal women include pelvic infections, uterine myomas or cysts, and ovarian cysts or tumors.

Postmenopausal women are unlikely to have many of these conditions, especially endometriosis, uterine myomas, ovarian cysts, or active pelvic infections. For them, atrophic vaginitis will be a more likely cause of deep as well as superficial pain, since shortening of the vagina may make vigorous thrusting uncomfortable. Other causes of deep pain for older women include tumors of the uterus or ovaries and scarring or adhesions from old operations or from chronic pelvic infections.

Sometimes scars that are very tender are quite small in size. They may be passed over or felt to be insignificant on a routine gynecological exam, but they may be quite painful on intercourse.

*Pelvic congestion syndrome.* This syndrome, another common cause of dyspareunia, is somewhat amorphous and difficult to define. You may have an aching and a heavy feeling in your pelvis, but your gynecologist may not be able to find anything wrong. You may find thrusting during intercourse very painful.

Women with this syndrome often turn out to have either varicose veins in their pelvis, swelling in the broad ligaments of the uterus, scars and stretching from childbearing, or possibly a retroflexed uterus. The uterus appears normal, but these women almost always lose the pain after hysterectomy.

## TREATMENT FOR DYSPAREUNIA

The good news about both superficial and deep pain with intercourse is that there usually is something physical causing it, and there's often something that can easily be done about it.

If your problem is due to vaginismus as the result of a previous cause for painful intercourse, and if that previous cause, such as a vaginal infection, is no longer present, excellent therapeutic results can be obtained with sexual therapy.

If either deep or superficial dyspareunia is due to atrophic vaginitis, the treatment is estrogen replacement. It can be fairly rapidly and spectacularly effective.

Most forms of infectious vaginitis, on the other hand, are treated with antibiotics.

Endometriosis may be treated either medically or surgically. Medically it is treated hormonally, either with danazol, an androgen derivative that supresses estrogen and causes the endometriosis patches to shrink and dry up, or by other hormonal treatments involving high-dose birth control pills or progesterone. Various types of surgical treatments remove the endometriosis directly. Among these is a new laser procedure that your gynecologist can best describe to you. Pelvic scars and adhesions are also usually treated surgically.

Keep in mind that while many of these conditions are treatable, they are often difficult to diagnose. It will take an understanding, intelligent doctor, as well as patience on both your parts, to help overcome them.

# 18

# Sex in Spite of Heart Trouble: Continue to Enjoy It

A simple and unpleasant fact of life is that, as we get older, we are more likely to suffer a heart attack or have to undergo a coronary bypass operation.

Men have many more heart problems than do women, and even a small one can have a traumatic effect on your sex life. A major cardiac problem such as a heart attack can cause you to lose your self-confidence and feel suddenly aged and afraid of exerting yourself. If this occurs, you may limit your sexual activity or develop impotence due to fear of causing another attack, due to angina or shortness of breath during sex, due to fatigue, or due to the side effects of medication.

A quarter of all men who have heart attacks give up sexual relations completely. Another 50 percent decrease the frequency of their sexual relations. Only the remaining quarter continue making love as often as before. This is really a shame. It's not necessary or desirable to give up your sexual life after a heart attack. Resuming sex is good for your confidence, for your feeling of masculinity, for your sense of being a successful person, and for your entire outlook on life. Eighty percent of postcoronary patients can resume their normal sexual activity without any serious risks. The other 20 percent don't have to abstain from sex, but simply need to adjust their lovemaking style according to their exercise tolerance.

If you have had a heart attack, you may worry: Will sex be too strenuous for me? Will my pulse rate go up too much? Will I get chest pain? Is sex safe for me? You may even worry about dying during intercourse. You may well wonder: Will lovemaking ever be the same again?

The actual facts are reassuring. Dying during sexual relations is actually an extremely rare occurrence. In a recent study of a large group of men with heart conditions who had died suddenly, less than *half of one percent* of them died during sex. Many more died in their sleep.

Moreover, most of those few who did die during sexual relations were having sex with someone other than their usual partner and had also consumed large amounts of alcohol. The added stress in a situation like this can increase heart rate and blood pressure to much higher than normal levels, placing an extra burden on the heart.

## HOW MUCH ENERGY CAN YOUR BODY SAFELY EXPEND?

Medical research has developed fairly sophisticated methods of measuring what your body can do and how much energy it can expend safely. Energy expenditure is measured in metabolic units called METS. For example, washing your hands uses about two METS, while doing carpentry work uses five to six METS. Champion athletes can get their performance up to about twenty METS.

If you are an average middle-aged man who's had an uncomplicated myocardial infarction, you can probably exert eight to nine METS without developing chest symptoms. Sexual activity requires a lot less than that. If you're having sex with your usual partner, you're likely to use about five METS during climax and about three to four METS during sexual play before and after climax. The energy level required for lovemaking is thus probably well within your capabilities. Of course, sex varies in the amount of energy expended according to the intensity and excitement of the situation, but if you can, say, walk up two flights of stairs or their equivalent, you are doing about five to six METS, and you can most likely handle the physical requirements of sexual relations without concern.

## SEX DOESN'T NECESSARILY PRODUCE YOUR PEAK PULSE RATE

Research on pulse rates during different activities has shown that ordinary daily activities often generate higher pulse rates than do sexual relations. In one study at Case Western Reserve School of Medicine, men wore portable cardiac monitors throughout the day to record their pulse rate continuously. During the course of an ordinary day, these men developed a maximum pulse rate of 120, on average. By contrast, the highest pulse rate they had during sexual relations averaged only about 117. Even this rate only lasted around ten to fifteen seconds—during orgasm.

One forty-eight-year-old attorney, for example, demonstrated higher pulse rates walking to court, arguing with another attorney, and presenting a case in the courtroom than he did during sexual relations. We don't usually think of practicing law as a physically strenuous occupation, but an ordinary lawyer may put less strain on his heart making love than he does when engaged in his profession.

## DISCOVER YOUR
## OWN EXERCISE TOLERANCE

Knowing that lovemaking will probably be a low risk for you will help you return to enjoying it as much as you did before your heart condition. Here are some steps you can take to reassure yourself:

*Get professional counseling.* Make sure that you get adequate counseling from your physician about what activities you can tolerate and which ones you can't. It's important to get your questions answered. Worry can create tension during lovemaking that may hamper enjoyment and may even cause you to have difficulty functioning.

Have your partner present if possible, so her questions can be answered too. She may be apprehensive about causing you harm or pain, and her anxiety may inhibit her response, not to mention yours.

Some doctors ignore the issue of sexual activity after a heart attack, most often because they feel uncomfortable talking about sex but sometimes because they have the misguided feeling that "at your age you shouldn't be worried about that."

If your doctor seems uncomfortable with the subject or doesn't seem to see it as a valid concern, ask to talk to another physician.

*Know your limits.* Lovemaking is a physical activity, a form of exercise like any other. So learn what your exercise tolerance is. With the help of a treadmill, as well as other tests, your doctor can evaluate you while checking your pulse rate and watching for arrhythmias. If you learn that you can tolerate a pulse rate of 140, for instance, and can climb several flights of stairs without getting anginal pain, then you probably can easily tolerate the exertion of sexual relations.

*Get yourself in shape.* Physical conditioning helps.
Many cardiac rehabilitation programs offer physical conditioning designed specifically for men recovering from myocardial infarctions. Getting in better condition will not only
make you feel physically stronger and more fit, it will also
mean that your heart won't have to work as hard during sex.

## HOW TO GO ABOUT
## RESUMING SEXUAL RELATIONS

You will probably be advised to wait two to six weeks after
your heart attack before resuming sexual relations. As much
as you may be looking forward to lovemaking, the prospect
may worry you too. These suggestions may make the transition easier:

*Start out slowly.* Alleviate some of your anxiety by
taking a week for sexual caressing and petting without attempting intercourse. In this way, you and your partner can
begin to enjoy lovemaking again without worrying about
performance or pain. Climaxing from manual or oral stimulation usually takes less exertion and causes less increase in
your heart rate and blood pressure than orgasm during intercourse does.

*Be comfortable and relaxed.* Resume sex in comfortable, familiar surroundings. Avoid trying sexual relations
when you're under high stress or anxiety from your job or
personal life. At these times your blood pressure and pulse
rate may be higher to begin with, bringing with them
higher risk.

*Find new, less taxing positions.* Experiment with your
partner to find less taxing positions for intercourse, such as
one in which the woman is on top or in which the two of

you are side to side. A comfortable alternative requiring minimal physical exertion is the spoon position, in which your partner lies on her side with her back toward you and you lie on your side behind her and insert your penis into her vagina from behind.

Lovemaking positions in which the man is on top, supporting his weight on his arms, do seem to require more energy than others. Remember, though, that the amount of energy used during lovemaking seems to be safe in most cases, whatever position you use. So if you are partial to the "man-on-top" position and don't experience discomfort, there's probably no real reason for you to change.

Remember, intercourse isn't required for you to enjoy lovemaking. If you feel tired or unenergetic, use oral or manual petting to pleasure your partner or bring her to climax, and she can do the same for you.

## FOR WOMEN WITH HEART CONDITIONS

Although considerably less common, women do suffer heart attacks too. If this has happened to you, much of the same advice I've given to men will apply as well. Your ordinary daily activities probably cause levels of exertion as high as those you would experience during sex, but it would be important to find out what your actual exercise tolerance is through a treadmill test—and to ask your doctor specific questions about how you can enjoy sex without undue cardiac stress. A conditioning program would also probably be helpful for you.

Resume sex gradually, with just caressing at first, and start with positions that are less physically taxing for you until you can judge what will cause discomfort.

## MEDICATIONS: SOME HELP,
## OTHERS MAY CAUSE PROBLEMS

Some medications that reduce painful heart symptoms can help you enjoy sex more. Others, also for your heart, can create sexual problems.

Some men *do* get anginal pain during sexual relations. In fact, this is one of the most common reasons that men give up sexual relations or develop impotence after a heart attack. If you do get angina during exertion, taking *nitroglycerine* or one of the longer-acting nitrates before making love may be helpful. Freeing your mind from the anticipation of pain will in turn make your lovemaking much more relaxed and enjoyable and will probably make it easier for you get erect.

*Beta blockers* such as Inderal cut down your maximum pulse rate during exertion and during intercourse and thereby decrease your chances of getting anginal pain. Unfortunately, these and some other medicines given to prevent arrhythmias can also have sexual side-effects when taken in large doses, resulting in loss of sexual drive or ability to get erect. If this should happen to you, ask your doctor about substituting another medication. It will depend on your overall cardiac condition.

## OTHER RECOMMENDATIONS

Most physicians recommend that you don't have intercourse just after eating a large meal or consuming large amounts of alcohol. The considerable energy and blood flow being expended in digestion makes less of both available for physical activity.

After a heart attack, many people become depressed and consumed with anxiety over their physical health. This loss of confidence and spirit can diminish sexual interest and desire. When you're worried and preoccupied, it's difficult to fully enjoy sex.

But resuming sexual activity in any form can actually help relieve some of your anxiety about your health. Sex is also an excellent reducer of anxiety in general and, whether you are a man or a woman, the feelings of closeness and intimacy achieved through satisfying lovemaking can impart a sense of well-being and fulfillment again.

If, after several weeks, you continue to feel depressed and unable to enjoy sex, it would be wise to ask your doctor to refer you to a psychiatrist who may be able to help you through this difficult period.

No one can guarantee that sex will be risk-free for you, and the risk can be higher at times of extra anxiety or excitement. It's a very small risk, though, taken for a very important reward. Every day you do many other things—like driving your car—that carry equal or greater risk. Life is meant to be lived, so if sex is important to you, go ahead and enjoy it and get the most out of it.

# 19

# Controlling Your Blood Pressure without Loss of Sexual Function

Some medications have side effects that very commonly cause erection difficulties in older men. *Antihypertensives,* prescribed for high blood pressure, are by far the most important and most commonly used medicines that cause sexual difficulty, and are responsible for an inordinately high number of sexual problems, especially in older men. Literally hundreds of men over forty have come to my clinic with erection difficulties due at least in part to antihypertensives. But those who need medication for high blood pressure *really need it* and have no choice but to take it, so it can be quite important to know which blood pressure medicines are most likely to cause such problems.

One of my most challenging tasks in preparing this book was interpreting the research on hypertension and sexuality. The information on this subject is confused and contradictory. Every expert has a somewhat different opinion about which medicines are the worst offenders and which are the least. Not only that, any study more than three or four years old is almost certain to be out of date; many of the medicines referred to are now rarely used and have been replaced by newer medications that weren't even available then. Definitive information on the incidence of sexual side-effects from these new medications is frequently unavailable.

What follows, then, is the result of my evaluation of the available studies, consolidated with my personal clinical experience and that of other physicians who work constantly with hypertensive patients.

## THE FIVE MAIN CLASSES OF BLOOD PRESSURE MEDICATIONS

Different medications can cause different sexual problems. Some are more likely to cause failure of erection, some create difficulties with ejaculation, and others are responsible for loss of desire. Still others can provoke two or more of these problems. While the most visible sexual side-effects, such as loss of erection, occur in men, it is not uncommon for women taking antihypertensive medications to suffer loss of sexual desire or difficulty with orgasm as well.

Five main groups of high-blood-pressure medications are currently in fairly wide use. First are the *diuretics,* of which the most commonly used are called thiazide diuretics. Among the second group, the *sympathetic blockers,* the most widely used are the beta blockers. The third main group of antihypertensives, the *vasodilators,* include alpha blockers and other medications whose mechanisms of action aren't well known. Group four, the *calcium channel-blockers,* usually prescribed for treatment of arrhythmia, are also used for their antihypertensive effect. Finally, a relatively new group of medicines, the *angiotensin converting enzyme inhibitors* (or ACE inhibitors), show a great deal of promise. A chart listing these medications by category can be found at the end of this chapter.

***The diuretics.*** Thiazide diuretics, the most widely used antihypertensive medications, are often the first ones tried. ("Thiazide" refers simply to their particular chemical structure.) Some of the most commonly used thiazide diuretics include *Hydrodiuril, Esidrix, Naqua, Enduron,* and *Oretic.* (The generic names can be found in the table on page 165.) *Maxzide* and *Dyazide,* two other commonly used medications, are combinations of a thiazide with another diuretic that conserves potassium. The diuretics generally work by increasing excretion of salt and water in your urine.

The overall consensus is that a relatively small percentage of men who use thiazide diuretics have trouble with erections and that ejaculation isn't affected at all.

A commonly used nonthiazide diuretic is *Lasix.* It has similar properties to the thiazides and also has a relatively low incidence of sexual side-effects. *Hygroton,* another nonthiazide diuretic, has a long duration of action. It apparently is also unlikely to cause sexual side-effects.

The only diuretic that has been known to cause sexual difficulties with some regularity is *Aldactone.* The sexual side-effects of this medication occur primarily in men. In high doses it seems to decrease the effective amount of the male sex hormone testosterone, and can cause impotence, breast enlargement, and loss of sex drive. It is now rarely used in the treatment of high blood pressure.

***The sympathetic nervous system blockers.*** The major sympathetic blockers used today are the beta blockers. ("Beta" blocker refers to the type of nerve-cell receptor that these medicines block to achieve their blood-pressure-lowering effect.)

Next to the thiazide diuretics, this group of medications is the most widely used in the treatment of hypertension. They tend to cause more sexual problems than the diuretics, but less difficulty than some of the earlier sympathetic blockers they replaced.

The problems caused by beta blockers are somewhat

## ANTIHYPERTENSIVE MEDICINES

| Category | Type | Brand Name | Generic Name |
|---|---|---|---|
| Diuretics | Thiazides | Hydrodiuril, Esidrix, Oretic<br>Naqua<br>Enduron | hydrochlorothiazide<br>trichlormethiazide<br>methyclothiazide |
| | Non-Thiazides | Lasix<br>Aldactone<br>Hygroton | furosemide<br>spironolactone<br>chlorthalidone |
| | Combinations | Dyazide, Maxzide | hydrochorothiazide and triamterene |
| Sympathetic Blockers | Beta Blockers | Inderal<br>Corgard<br>Tenormin<br>Lopressor<br>Blockadren | propranolol<br>nadolol<br>atenolol<br>metoprolol<br>timolol |
| | Alpha and Beta Blockers | Trandate | labetolol |
| | Others | Aldomet<br>Ismelin<br>Serpasil and others<br>Catapres | alpha-methyldopa<br>guanethidine<br>reserpine<br>clonidine |
| Vasodilators | | Apresoline<br>Minipress | hydralazine<br>prazosin |
| Calcium Channel Blockers | | Procardia<br>Isoptin, Calan<br>Cardizem | nifedipine<br>verapamil<br>diltiazem |
| Angiotensin Converting Enzyme Inhibitors | | Capoten<br>Vasotec | captopril<br>enalapril |

dependent on the size of the dose. If you can get away with a lower dose, you'll have less chance of having sexual problems, so it's important to keep your weight down, to exercise, and to avoid salt.

Two of the beta blockers, *Lopressor* and *Tenormin,* are referred to as "selective" beta blockers. They block certain beta nerve-cell receptors more than others, which theoretically should make them less liable to cause impotence than other beta blockers. Unfortunately, though, this distinction doesn't seem to be clear in actual practice.

Perhaps a more important difference is that two of the beta blockers, *Inderal* and *Lopressor,* pass more easily into the brain and therefore may be more likely to cause depression and loss of sexual desire. The other two frequently used medications in this group, *Tenormin* and *Corgard,* may thus be the best bets in the beta-blocker group, but the distinction is not great. Sometimes one beta blocker will cause trouble and another one won't, for no clear-cut reason.

The beta blocker *Trandate* has alpha-blocking qualities as well. Some researchers feel that this property may prevent some of the sexual side-effects evidenced by other beta blockers.

Besides the beta-blockers, other sympathetic blockers include *Aldomet, Ismelin, reserpine (Serpasil,* etc.), and *Catapres.* These medicines, once widely used for hypertension, have now fallen out of favor because they produce many more side effects than do the beta blockers.

*Aldomet* frequently inhibits sexual function. The number of patients taking it who have reported sexual problems, ranges up to 40 percent, depending on the dose. The problems include impotence, loss of desire, and inability to ejaculate for men, and loss of desire and difficulty in achieving orgasm for women.

*Ismelin* in high doses inhibits ejaculation for up to 60 percent of the men using it. Impotence is seen less frequently.

*Reserpine* can cause depression, sedation, and loss of desire in both sexes, even in low doses. Impotence is a fairly common side effect.

Ten to 20 percent of men taking *Catapres* report difficulty with erection. Loss of sexual desire may be seen in both sexes, as well as inability to ejaculate in men and inability to achieve orgasm in women.

**The vasodilators.** This group of antihypertensives has few sexual side-effects. Once commonly used, it is being replaced by calcium channel blockers and ACE inhibitors, which have even fewer side effects.

*Apresoline* is one of the more commonly prescribed vasodilators. It usually must be administered in combination with beta blockers and sometimes with a diuretic as well. By itself it seems to have almost no negative effects on sexual function for either men or women.

*Minipress,* another vasodilator, seems to have very few sexual side-effects and can more often be used alone. Unfortunately, it isn't able to control blood pressure for everyone, especially when given alone, and some people develop other side effects not related to sex.

**The calcium channel-blockers.** This relatively new group of medications helps control arrhythmia as well as high blood pressure. When these medications work, they are wonderful, causing few sexual side-effects, as far as we can tell at present. Unfortunately, they are effective in controlling the blood pressure of only about one patient in three. If they do work for you, they are a best bet.

Some of the most common calcium channel-blockers are *Procardia, Isoptin, Calan,* and *Cardizem.*

**The ACE inhibitors.** The angiotension converting enzyme inhibitors (ACE inhibitors) are a new class of antihypertensives that are very well tolerated by most people. They have almost no side effects, sexual or otherwise.

As with nearly any medication, however, there is a

down side, and in this case it's that the very rare, one-in-a-thousand side effect that does occur can be very serious. The first ACE inhibitor introduced, *Capoten,* can suppress white blood cells. This happens quite rarely but can be life-threatening if it does occur. A newer ACE inhibitor, *Vasotec,* seems to be even safer than Capoten and can be given only once a day. These medications have great promise and are gradually becoming a first choice in treating hypertension.

## BEST BETS FOR CONTROLLING BLOOD PRESSURE WITH MINIMAL SIDE EFFECTS

No formula for treating blood pressure is right for everyone; the choices are now too wide and must be individualized for every patient. Nonetheless, what I can do here is present a rational course of action that can serve as a guideline for a man who wishes to control his blood pressure while conserving his sexual function.

1. *Weight loss, salt restriction,* and *exercise* may be enough to control your blood pressure without medication. At any rate, these are steps you can take yourself that will help you to minimize the amount of medication you will need.

2. If you require medication, *a calcium channel-blocker* or *Vasotec* would be a good place to start. Either of these may control your blood pressure by itself with few side effects of any kind, sexual or otherwise.

3. If the calcium channel-blocker or ACE inhibitor does not control your blood pressure, a *thiazide diuretic* can be added. This combination would still be quite unlikely to cause any sexual problems.

4. If this combination of medicines doesn't work either, try substituting *Minipress* for the calcium channel-blocker.

5. If the hypertension is still not controlled, you will probably have to add a *beta blocker*. Remember that while beta
blockers do cause sexual side-effects for a substantial
number of patients, the number for whom beta blockers
*don't* cause side effects is far greater still. And if one beta
blocker causes sexual difficulty, another may not.

## THE MEDICINES WITH
## THE WORST RECORDS

These seem to be Ismelin, Catapres, reserpine, Aldactone (in
men), and Aldomet. Inderal seems to be the worst among the
beta blockers, but we can't discount the possibility that this
is just because it has been around longest and we know the
most about it.

## DON'T BE FRIGHTENED OFF

Hypertension is a major health problem and causes a greatly
increased incidence of heart attacks, strokes, and kidney
disease. But because it's a silent disease, people don't feel ill
while the disease is progressing—until it reaches a very serious state. Since patients don't feel sick in the early and
middle stages of hypertensive illness, they tend to be impatient with the side effects of the medications that treat it.

   It's important for you *not* to be frightened off by the
sexual side-effects of antihypertensive medications. The
frequency of such side effects is low with most of them and
not commonplace with *any* of those routinely used today.
Remember that a 5 percent incidence of sexual problems
with a particular medicine means that 95 percent of the
people taking it *don't* have sexual problems. Moreover, drug-
related side effects, if they do occur, are reversible within a
week or two after discontinuing the medicine.

   We also know that a combination of different medicines and different classes of medicine allow for a lower dose of each and probably result in fewer overall side effects.

Even if one particular medicine does cause sexual side-effects, another one may not. Frequently a change to another medication, even one from the same group, can overcome the problem. If your doctor is too rigid to do this or doesn't seem to care about your sexual difficulties, try another doctor.

Don't automatically assume that the blood pressure medicine you're taking is causing whatever sexual difficulty you may be having. Other very common causes of sexual difficulty that need to be evaluated include anxiety, stress, alcohol, smoking, diabetes, arteriosclerosis, other illnesses, and other medications.

While I suggest various medications in this chapter, remember that your personal physician knows your case best and is best equipped to determine which medicines have the best chance of working for you, in the safest possible combinations.

# 20

# Prescription Medicines that Can Block Sexual Response

As we reach the years over forty, we tend to be more vulnerable to sexual side-effects from medications in general. This is partly because as we get older we have to take more medicines, and partly because at this age our sexual responses, especially those of males, become more fragile and more easily thrown off course by medication side-effects.

While some medications can cause women to have decreased sexual desire and impaired response, this condition is certainly less common than for men. This may partly be a result of women being less open about reporting sexual side-effects, and partly because sexual impairment in women is harder to measure than a penis that doesn't rise; but, unquestionably, a major part of the sexual disparity is due to the fact that women's sexual responses are not affected as much by aging as men's are. This means that men over forty, with erection ability already a bit compromised, are simply more likely to be pushed past the threshold by a medication side-effect.

Sexual function is a very complex process, and almost

any drug that affects bodily processes can affect it on occasion. Rather than try to list here every medicine that can possibly cause sexual difficulty, I'll briefly run through those classes of drugs in which sexual side-effects are most likely to be seen.

## THE ANTIDEPRESSANTS

*Tricyclic antidepressants* and related compounds are the most commonly used medications in the treatment of depression. Some of the widely known brand names include Elavil, Endep, Tofranil, Norpramin, Pamelor, Vivactil, Surmontil, Sinequan, and Ludiomil (generics: amitriptyline, imipramine, desipramine, nortriptyline, protriptyline, trimipramine, doxepin, and maprotiline).

These medications can cause sedation and decreased sexual desire in both men and women, as well as impotence in men. Research on the frequency of these side effects is incomplete, but indications are that they occur in a fairly small minority of patients. Impaired ejaculation has been reported, but it is even less frequent.

Assessments of the sexual side-effects of antidepressants are complicated by the fact that depression itself may frequently cause lack of sexual desire or impotence. In fact, depression probably causes these symptoms considerably more frequently than does antidepressant medication. The antidepressants, by treating the depression, actually help to restore sexual desire and sexual functioning in many instances.

For this reason, I certainly wouldn't advise avoiding antidepressant medications because of the possibility of sexual side-effects. If you need them, it's important to take them. And if one of them does cause sexual trouble, another may not. Desyrel (trazodone), in particular, is unlikely to cause erection difficulty and may even help—although it may not be quite as strong an antidepressant as some of the others and must be used with care in patients with preexisting heart disease.

The *monoamine oxidase (MAO) inhibitors,* another class of antidepressants, are less frequently used because they can have more severe side effects—but they sometimes work when a tricyclic won't, and they are more effective for treating certain conditions. Two of the more commonly used MAO inhibitors are Nardil and Parnate (generics: phenelzine and tranylcypromine).

The MAO inhibitors are less likely to affect sexual desire and erection, but they seem to cause impaired ejaculation fairly frequently. Inability to reach orgasm in women has also been reported. If inability to ejaculate does occur, it usually can be overcome by decreasing the dose. In other cases, it just clears up by itself after a few weeks.

## THE ANTIHISTAMINES

Almost everyone has used antihistamines for treatment of colds, hay fever, allergies, or sinus trouble. These medications can be very useful, but their anticholinergic property that dries up your nose (which is the reason you take it) may also cause drying of vaginal secretions, and even impotence. Older men and women are particularly vulnerable to these side effects, as some postmenopausal women may already have some decreased lubrication, and older men may have some erectile fragility.

If you are taking an antihistamine temporarily for a cold and you find that your penis just won't get erect, don't be alarmed. This side effect will disappear when you stop taking the medication.

## ULCER MEDICATIONS

Tagamet (cimetidine) is a very commonly used and effective medication for the treatment of ulcers. It decreases the secretion of stomach acid and has antihistaminic properties. Unfortunately, it also has antisexual effects on men, because it blocks the effect of the androgens, or male hormones.

*Zantac* (ranitidine) is just as successful in treating ulcers but doesn't have antiandrogen effects. If Tagamet has caused sexual problems for you, you might ask your doctor about Zantac.

## OTHER MISCELLANEOUS DRUGS

*Major tranquilizers* are prescribed primarily for serious psychiatric conditions, but they are also occasionally given in low doses for such symptoms as severe anxiety. Such tranquilizers as Thorazine, Stelazine, Trilafon, Mellaril, and Haldol have sedating effects, which can interfere with sexual desire, and anticholinergic effects, which can interfere with erection. They may also raise the levels of prolactin, a pituitary hormone, and may interfere with male sexual hormones in other ways. Tranquilizers have been known to cause loss of sexual desire, impotence, and, occasionally, impaired ejaculation or orgasm. Again, older men and women can be more vulnerable to these side effects.

Common *antianxiety medications* such as Valium, Librium, and Xanax may also decrease sexual desire, especially when taken in high doses. Other medications that occasionally cause sexual difficulty include *muscle relaxants* such as Flexeril, Norflex, Norgesic, and Disipal; *medications for Parkinson's disease* such as Cogentin, Artane, Kemadrin, and Akineton; and such *miscellaneous medicines* as Lanoxin, Dilantin, Reglan, Flagyl, Indocin, and Atromid-S. The reason that some of these medicines affect sexual response is obscure.

(Generic names for *major tranquilizers:* chlorpromazine, trifluoperazine, perphenazine, thioridazine, haloperidol; for *antianxiety medications:* diazepam, chlordiazepoxide, alprazolam; for *muscle relaxants:* cyclobenzaprine, orphenadrine; for *Parkinson's disease medications:* benztropine, trihexyphenidyl, procyclidine, biperiden; and for *miscellaneous medicines:* digoxin, phenytoin, metoclopramide, metronidazole, indomethacin, clofibrate.)

Again, remember that just because you're taking one of these medicines doesn't mean you are likely to have sexual difficulties. And if you are taking one of these medicines and do have sexual difficulties, there's no assurance that the medicine is necessarily responsible for the problem, unless the problem clearly started shortly after you began taking the drug.

# 21

# Drinking, Smoking, Drugs, and Sex Over 40

You may get the feeling that there is a constant barrage of voices telling you that some of your favorite things, such as alcohol and smoking, are bad for you. Much as I regret adding my voice to others, I must. If you drink or smoke heavily, this chapter may be a real downer for you. It may, indeed, be quite upsetting. But unpleasant as this information is, it's crucial for you to hear it, if you want to maintain a good active sexual life.

## WHAT ARE THE LONG-TERM EFFECTS OF ALCOHOL CONSUMPTION?

At some time or other, you've probably had a drink or two before a lovemaking episode and felt that it helped you to relax and to be more uninhibited. But what about the effects of three or four drinks—or more—on your sexual ability when you're over forty? And what are the effects of chronic or heavy alcohol use?

I wish that I could tell you that alcohol is perfectly safe

and won't cause you any sexual trouble. Unfortunately, that's simply not the way it is. All the medical evidence indicates that alcohol, in large amounts, can be extremely destructive to your sexual life. A pint of hard liquor per day, or an equivalent amount of alcohol as wine or beer, can cause complete loss of sexual function in as few as five to eight years. As many as 80 percent of men who drink very heavily are reported to develop impotence, sterility, or loss of sexual desire.

Heavy drinking seems to be especially toxic to the male sex glands, the testicles. Over a long period of time, it destroys the cells and leaves you with atrophic (shrunken) testicles. One of your testicles' main functions is to produce the male hormone testosterone. As we described in chapter 2, testosterone regulates sexual desire and potency. Overuse of alcohol for a long period of time can greatly decrease production of testosterone. This may result in loss of sexual desire and even impotence.

The testicles also produce sperm. As excessive alcohol consumption gradually destroys your testicles, it causes you to have a lowered sperm count, which will eventually make you sterile and thus unable to father a child. This may still be an important consideration for many over-forty men.

## HOW ALCOHOL LOWERS YOUR MALE HORMONE LEVELS

Alcohol actually decreases your working levels of testosterone in three ways.

First of all, it decreases the production of testosterone in your testicles, as just described. Second, it alters your metabolism by increasing the speed at which testosterone is broken down in your body. In doing so, it changes your body's hormone balance. Men who drink very heavily have less male hormone and more female hormone than normal. (Men normally have small amounts of female hormones in their bodies, just as women have small amounts of male hormones.) Third, alcohol increases the percentage of testosterone in your blood that's tightly bound to protein. This means that less of it is free and able to act. Thus, not only is there a reduced amount of testosterone produced, but part of what is produced isn't usable.

Besides its effects on the testicles, alcohol damages your liver, and this damage helps to produce the hormonal imbalance with excess female hormones. Alcohol may also have toxic effects on the areas of the brain that help regulate sex hormones, disrupting the production of the pituitary hormones, which stimulate the testicles to produce testosterone and sperm.

Finally, men who drink very heavily may develop antibodies against their own sperm and testicles. These antibodies can lead to testicular damage and infertility.

Remembering that testosterone levels usually decrease with age anyway—and that your liver gradually loses some of its efficiency even without alcohol—you can see how heavy drinking after forty can be even more debilitating than when you were younger.

## IS THE DAMAGE PERMANENT?
## WILL IT HELP IF I STOP DRINKING?

Two types of damage result from chronic alcohol abuse. The first is the change in your body's biochemistry, which causes you to have lowered levels of male hormone. This change can be reversed if you stop drinking, although it will take some time.

The second is the permanent destruction of the cells of the testicles and liver. This probably takes heavy drinking over a long period of time, but once it occurs, it's not reversible. Once testicular and liver cells are gone, they won't return.

So while many men can regain sexual function within

several months if they quit drinking, for others it may be too late. It seems to depend on the amount of cell damage in the testicles and liver that has already occurred. Men with atrophic testicles and damaged livers are unlikely to have a return of sexual function from just stopping drinking, because these organs are already irreversibly damaged. But the earlier you catch it and stop drinking, the better your chances. Even if you don't get a full return of function, at least you will prevent further damage. Because enough liver damage won't just cause impotence—it will kill you.

## EVEN ONE EPISODE OF EXCESSIVE DRINKING CAN AFFECT YOU

The negative results of alcohol on sexuality don't affect only those who happen to be alcoholics. Early signs of damage can be seen after a single episode of excessive drinking. Enough alcohol to produce a hangover can cause temporarily decreased testosterone levels even in normal, healthy men.

Alcohol has other immediate effects. It serves as a depressant to the central nervous system, and as such the first thing it does in small doses is decrease your inhibitions and allow you to relax. But in higher doses, it *deadens* your nervous system. This means that you become less sensitive and more sedated. Alcohol thus numbs the reflex pathways that your body depends on for sexual response. It ends up causing sexual failure.

This deadening effect of high doses of alcohol on sexuality has been well proven. For example, the more alcohol that men have consumed in the previous twenty-four hours, the more their nighttime erections decrease in size and frequency—and the more alcohol they consume before watching sex films, the fewer and smaller erections they're measured to have. This is the opposite of what men often expect, which is that alcohol will help them to get erect.

The immediate sexual-suppressing effect from a single

dose of alcohol can cause a man lasting sexual difficulties. For example, after a party at which he had consumed a particularly large amount of alcohol, Bill W., a patient of mine, came home and attempted to have sex with his wife. Unfortunately, due to the alcohol, he completely failed to get an erection. The next morning he remembered what had happened, and he worried for the next two days about his failure. When he tried again, his worry caused another failure and more worry. His single episode of alcohol-created impotence snowballed into the prolonged period of sexual difficulty that eventually brought him to my office.

This pattern of alcohol-induced failure, leading to anxiety about performance and more failures, is not at all uncommon, and it can affect women as well. After heavy alcohol consumption causes failure of arousal or orgasm, a woman may consciously watch her response and try harder to get aroused the next time. This usually has the opposite effect and can get her into the same vicious circle of anxiety and sexual difficulty that Bill W. suffered from.

## MEN OVER FORTY ARE
## PARTICULARLY VULNERABLE

Older men are especially susceptible to the detrimental effects of alcohol on potency. As you age, your erection reflex gets more fragile, and an amount of alcohol that would have caused no problem in prior years may be enough to tip the balance to loss of function. When you were younger, your erection reflex was so strong that you could get erect under almost any circumstances, in spite of the deadening effects of alcohol. Now you simply don't have the reserve that you once had. Your testosterone levels have declined with age, and the vascular supply to your penis isn't as strong as it used to be. You can't afford to have your testosterone levels further lowered by alcohol. You also can't afford to deaden your senses with alcohol and expect to function well. You need to give yourself all the advantage you can, instead of letting alcohol make it difficult or impossible for you to get erect.

## AND WOMEN?

The effects of alcohol on women in many ways parallel those on men. Immediately, a small amount of alcohol, such as one or two drinks, may relax your inhibitions, which may allow you to feel more sexually aroused. However, after three to five drinks you may have considerable difficulty in climaxing because of the deadening effects of alcohol on your nervous system. With much more alcohol, you will likely become quite intoxicated, fall asleep, or pass out.

Chronic alcohol abuse is toxic to the ovaries, the female sexual glands, in the same way that it's toxic to the testicles. Damage to the ovaries causes menstrual abnormalities, lack of ovulation, and signs of estrogen deprivation. The lack of estrogen can cause atrophy of the breasts, uterus, and vaginal walls, along with loss of lubrication. Alcoholic women also suffer from chronic liver disease, premature aging, and early menopause. Masters and Johnson report that 30 to 60 percent of alcoholic women claim difficulty in becoming sexually aroused, impaired orgasm, and other sexual problems.

## DOES THIS MEAN
## I SHOULDN'T DRINK AT ALL?

You may be wondering, "What does this mean to me? Do I have to stop drinking completely? Will an occasional drink or two cause me any trouble? How long will it take for heavy drinking to cause problems for me sexually?"

It should be emphasized that most of the data referred to here involve studies done on chronic heavy drinkers. These are not skid-row alcoholics, though. I see people like them with sexual problems every day—"ordinary people" who live with their families, go to work every day (or almost every day), but who "like to drink." If you are one of these people, this kind of damage could be happening to you.

There's considerable individual variation in susceptibility to damage from alcohol. Not everyone who drinks a pint a day for six or seven years will become impotent. On the other hand, some people may experience loss of function from much smaller amounts, or after drinking for a shorter time.

While there is evidence that a large amount of drinking, even on a single occasion, will cause a temporary drop in testosterone, there is no indication that one or two drinks a couple of times a week will cause any loss of sexual function.

What I'd advise, therefore, is very simple:

1. If you've had decreased sexual function and you've been drinking moderate to heavy amounts, try discontinuing for at least three or four months to see if your function returns.

2. If you've been drinking heavily and you haven't yet suffered a loss of function, you're in luck: You can cut down or quit now before it's too late.

3. If you're concerned about your sexual function, I suggest you limit yourself to a maximum of one or two drinks before a sexual encounter, and keep your total alcohol consumption light.

# How Smoking Cigarettes Can Suppress Your Sexual Functioning

The effects of cigarette smoking on sexual functioning have not been as thoroughly studied as have the effects of alcohol. There is little known, for example, about the effect of smoking on female sexual response. There is, however, considerable evidence that smoking has damaging effects on a man's erection ability, both immediate and long term. In fact, Dr. Irwin Goldstein, an important impotence researcher at Boston University Medical School, recently stated that "Smoking may be the most important risk factor for erection problems." He noted that about 80% of the impotent men he treats are smokers. A large proportion of impotent men in my own practice are smokers as well.

Smoking as few as two high-nicotine cigarettes before sexual arousal can cause decreased erection as well as slower arousal, even in healthy young men. This effect is probably caused by the immediate vasoconstrictive effects of nicotine —meaning that nicotine constricts the small blood vessels in your penis, cutting down the blood supply and thereby delaying or preventing erections.

There is also evidence that impotent men are much more likely to be smokers than the general population, and the incidence of *heavy* smoking among impotent men is much greater than in the general population. Heavy smokers also tend to have decreased blood pressure in their penises, confirming the impaired blood supply that contributes to impaired erections. The evidence shows that men who have smoked the longest and have smoked the most cigarettes per day have the lowest penile blood pressures.

Overall, this implies that cigarette smoking is clearly a risk factor in producing impotence as well as many other medical problems. The way it affects men seems to be largely vascular, by narrowing and obstructing the blood vessels needed to produce erection.

What if you quit smoking? A recent study from Washington Hospital Center, which was published in the journal *Urology*, examined men who were impotent due to what the researchers felt were vascular causes. Some of them had diabetes. In others, there was no clear-cut cause for their impotence except for the fact that they smoked a pack and a half or more of cigarettes per day.

The investigators felt that there was good evidence that smoking caused constriction of the blood vessels and that it was contributing to the men's sexual problems. The men were asked to discontinue smoking for a trial period. It was found that 35 percent of these men with proven impotence had their problems reversed within six weeks—by simply not smoking for that period of time.

It's clear that stopping smoking won't reverse impotence in everyone. But it is striking that more than one-third of these men experienced a return of erections *with no other treatment* than stopping smoking.

So if you value your continued sexual function, keep in mind that there is considerable evidence that by smoking a pack or more of cigarettes per day you are endangering it. The longer you smoke and the more you smoke, the more you're probably endangering yourself. The sexual-suppressing effect probably occurs because nicotine constricts the blood vessels and smoking increases hardening of the arteries (arteriosclerosis). I'm well aware that smoking is a very difficult addiction to break and that quitting isn't easy, but endangering your sexual life by smoking isn't pleasant to contemplate either.

Certainly the relationship between drinking, smoking, and sexuality is complex and interwoven with social factors and attitudes. Cutting down on drinking and quitting smoking won't guarantee that your sexual response will never be impaired, or that it will be restored if you are currently having trouble. It again comes down to the fact that, as you get older, it makes sense to maximize your chances for good sexual functioning by eliminating factors that can potentially cause major impairment—and alcohol abuse and smoking are definitely in that category.

# "Recreational" Drugs

The use of recreational drugs has become all too common in our society—even, in some cases, among men and women over forty. I would be remiss if I didn't mention some of the sexual effects—and dangers—of the most common of these drugs.

The short-term sexual effects of psychoactive drugs are extremely variable. They depend a lot on the social setting and on the expectation of the user. For the most part, however, the occasional use of small amounts of such drugs as marijuana, cocaine, and amphetamines may be experienced as reducing inhibitions and increasing sexual sensitivity. As with alcohol, though, the ingestion of larger amounts of these drugs tends to interfere with such sexual responses as erection, ejaculation, and female orgasm—while chronic, steady use tends to cause progressive loss of sexual desire for both sexes, resulting in inability to reach erection or ejaculation for men and inability to reach orgasm for women.

Heroin and other narcotic opiates are sexual suppressants in almost any dose.

*Marijuana.* Marijuana is commonly thought to have an aphrodisiaclike effect. About 80 percent of both men and women in a large study by Masters and Johnson reported that marijuana enhanced their enjoyment of sex. More specific questions, however, determined that what was enhanced was sensory perception and the feeling of relationship with one's partner. Actual sexual functions, such as erection ability, ejaculation, vaginal lubrication, or female orgasm, were not improved—in fact, they were actually interfered with in many cases, especially when high doses had been taken. As with alcohol, a small amount may have released inhibitions, but larger amounts tended to cause inability to get erect, ejaculate, or reach orgasm.

With chronic use, marijuana is an antisexual drug. In animals it decreases copulation activity, suppresses the production of sperm and testosterone in males, and prevents ovulation in females. In humans it definitely causes marked suppression of testosterone levels and decreases sperm counts. It can cause loss of sexual desire, inability to ejaculate and impotence in men who are chronic users, and loss of desire and inability to reach orgasm in women. In one study of daily users, one out of five was impotent.

*Cocaine.* Highly valued in the drug culture as a sexual stimulant, cocaine reduces inhibitions and apparently can increase sexual desire in both men and women in the short run. It also increases tactile sensation and can prolong intercourse by delaying ejaculation.

With chronic usage, however, there is first an inability for men to ejaculate or women to reach climax, then loss of male erection ability and female arousal, and finally, after a few months, complete loss of sexual interest for both sexes. This is probably due to the drug's depletion of dopamine, a specific neurotransmitter in the nervous system.

The initial effects of cocaine can be seductive, but this is a very dangerous drug. A single dose can be fatal. Besides this, it is highly, highly addictive. People who think they will be just social users can become compulsively addicted, ruining their marriages, losing their jobs, and bankrupting themselves. Beware of cocaine.

*Amphetamines ("speed").* Much less scientific data are available on the effects of amphetamines on sex. Like cocaine, however, these are central-nervous-system stimulants. Anecdotal reports indicate that amphetamines have many of the same initial effects as cocaine, as well as similar long-term dangers and side effects.

*Opiates and narcotics (heroin).* The sexual story on opiates is pretty clear-cut. Opiates will decrease sexual desire and function in almost 100 percent of regular users. Both men and women lose the ability to become aroused. Men develop impotence. Women can't climax. Testosterone and pituitary sex hormones are depressed in men. Women stop ovulating and develop amenorrhea. Opiates are definitely a sexual downer.

# 22

# Prostate Problems, Sex, and the Older Man

With aging, some prostate trouble is almost inevitable for most men. Unfortunately, though, when many men think of prostate trouble they think of frightening operations, loss of sexual function, and embarrassing urinary symptoms. You'll be glad to hear that it doesn't have to be that way at all. In fact, you can continue to have good sex indefinitely in spite of prostate trouble.

Prior to age forty, your prostate gland is likely to cause you little difficulty besides an occasional prostate infection. However, by your fifties or sixties, you will probably start noticing changes in your urinary and sexual functioning caused by enlargement of your prostate gland.

Your prostate is a small gland located between your bladder and the base of your penis. It actually fits like a small doughnut around your urethra (the passage you urinate through) where your urethra leaves your bladder. This area is called the bladder neck. The rectum is right behind it, so your doctor can easily feel your prostate during a rectal exam.

The prostate is normally about one and a half to two inches in size, and it weighs about half an ounce. Enlarged prostates can be fifteen times this size and weigh as much as half a pound.

Only men have a prostate gland. It grows to its full size at puberty, under the stimulation of your male sex hormones, just like your other sex organs. It is composed, for the most part, of glandular tissue with a fibrous and muscular capsule.

Your prostate is constantly at work producing enzymes, hormonelike substances, and, most important, the alkaline fluid that comprises most of your ejaculation. This fluid helps the sperm to swim once they reach the vagina.

A small amount of this prostatic fluid is usually voided every time you urinate so it won't build up in your prostate. Your prostate produces more fluid than usual when you are sexually excited, to ensure an adequate supply for ejaculation. If you go for a long period of time with frequent episodes of excitement but no ejaculation, your prostate may become painfully congested with fluid. While not dangerous, this can be very uncomfortable.

## PROSTATIC ENLARGEMENT, OR BPH

For reasons that nobody understands for sure, most men's prostates begin to grow again at about the age of forty or fifty. This causes prostatic enlargement, also called benign prostatic hypertrophy or BPH. BPH represents the enlargement of the glandular, fibrous, and muscular tissue inside the capsule of your prostate. It doesn't spread into other tissue, it's not invasive, and it's not cancer.

BPH really isn't any danger in itself, but your enlarged prostate may start to obstruct your urinary passage, which passes through it. In extreme cases, the obstruction may completely block your urine outflow. Since BPH starts very gradually and causes symptoms only if it obstructs your urine, you can have it for a long time and never even know it.

The symptoms caused by blockage due to BPH include some or all of the following: a need to urinate more often than usual during the night, difficulty in starting your urinary stream, slowness and weakness of your stream, a need to urinate frequently and with great urgency, painful or uncomfortable urination, dribbling of urine after urination, and passing small amounts of blood in your urine or ejaculate.

The good news is that BPH usually doesn't interfere with your *sexual* activity except perhaps for a slight decrease in the force of your ejaculation. When BPH is accompanied by congestion, in rare cases it may cause erection difficulty, but this is very unlikely.

What causes BPH isn't clear. Male hormones have to be present for the prostate to enlarge, but they were present in much higher amounts when you were younger. Dietary factors may be related to BPH. Japanese men on a traditional fish diet with low cholesterol have a low incidence of BPH and of prostatic cancer. When they come to this country or switch to a diet high in saturated fats, the same men get more prostatic enlargement and more prostate cancer.

Some doctors feel that the body nutrient zinc may play a factor. Zinc is highly concentrated in the prostate and seems to play a role in its proper function. Some physicians believe that the prostate enlarges in response to low zinc levels, the same way that the thyroid enlarges in response to low iodine levels.

There is considerable evidence that older men can develop zinc deficiency, so some people deduce that taking supplementary zinc in doses of about 50 mg per day may help prevent prostate enlargement. It's very difficult to find any scientific studies proving this—or disproving it either, for that matter. Many men take zinc for their prostate because they and their doctors hope that it will be beneficial, but it's not a medically proven treatment at this time.

## PROSTATE INFECTION

Prostate infection, called *prostatitis,* is a common illness in men, and it may occur at any age.

*Acute bacterial prostatitis* usually strikes with the sudden onset of fever, chills, nausea, vomiting, inability to start urinating, or painful, burning urination. You may feel as if you have to urinate with great urgency and frequency, but you may produce only small amounts of urine. You may also have rectal pain and low back pain. Because it can be quite serious, it's important to consult with your doctor as soon as possible after the onset of symptoms.

Once an infection gets into the prostate it's difficult to completely eliminate it. The prostate doesn't empty well. It's hard for antibiotics to get into this area, and it's hard for prostatic fluid to get out. Little pockets of infection remain resistent to treatment.

*Chronic recurring prostatitis,* which may or may not start with an acute infection, can thus be very frustrating for you and your doctor alike. The symptoms of chronic prostatitis are more vague than the symptoms of the acute infection. They can include aching in the area between your scrotum and your rectum, low back pain, and burning with urination.

Treatment for prostatitis varies. It's easy to control acute bacterial prostatitis with antibiotics, but it's very difficult to completely eradicate it if it develops into the chronic variety. It may require two weeks in some cases, while in others it may take six months. The infection may seemingly disappear, then come back over and over again.

Some simple treatments that can relieve the symptoms of chronic prostatitis include sitz baths (where the heat seems to have a beneficial effect by increasing blood supply), and prostatic massage, which helps relieve the symptoms by draining fluid from the prostatic ducts.

Zinc may also play a role in the treatment of chronic prostatitis. Prostatic secretions normally have an antibacterial action that helps to prevent prostate infections. The effectiveness of this antibacterial response seems proportional to the levels of zinc in the secretions. Men who have chronic, recurring prostate infections have been found to have extremely low prostatic zinc levels.

The urologists I consulted say there isn't any definitive scientific evidence that zinc supplementation prevents recurrences of prostatic infections, but they believe empirically that it does help some men. Several of my patients have told me that taking zinc supplements has eliminated recurrences of their chronic prostate infections.

Chronic prostatitis can cause a particular sexual difficulty: Men with this condition may sometimes experience an excruciatingly painful spasm of the prostate muscles when they ejaculate. If a man has a number of painful ejaculations, he may develop difficulty in obtaining erections or ejaculating because of his conditioned reflex against the pain.

## CONGESTIVE PROSTATITIS

Another type of prostatitis, called *congestive prostatitis, prostatosis,* or *prostatodynia,* doesn't involve any apparent infection and isn't accompanied by fever or chills. Aside from this, many of the symptoms—frequency, urgency, and inability to start the urinary stream—can resemble the symptoms of infectious prostatitis.

Congestive prostatitis means your prostate is filled with excessive fluid. There are a number of possible causes. First of all, you may have experienced repeated sexual stimulation without ejaculation, causing the production of extra prostatic fluid that hasn't been expelled. (This doesn't mean, however, that you should try to force yourself to ejaculate every time you have sex. Now that you're over forty or fifty, you actually don't have the need to climax each time, because your prostate doesn't make as much prostatic fluid. When your ejaculation fluid builds up, you probably will ejaculate without much difficulty.)

A second possible cause of prostate congestion is constant vibration, which apparently also stimulates the production of prostatic fluid. Motorcyclists and truck drivers, for example, often develop this uncomfortable congestion.

Third, some doctors feel that BPH, or prostatic enlargement, may encourage prostatic congestion by making it difficult for prostatic fluid to drain.

Finally, prostatic congestion can develop in some men without any known cause.

Prostatic congestion can be relieved by ejaculation. A substitute for this is prostatic massage, which milks the excess fluid out of the prostate gland.

The symptoms of all types of prostatitis, as well as BPH, can suddenly worsen if you eat large amounts of very spicy foods, drink large amounts of coffee or alcohol, or sit on a cold surface for a long time.

Neither infectious nor congestive prostatitis increases your chances of getting cancer of the prostate or of getting BPH, as far as anyone knows.

## CANCER OF THE PROSTATE

Cancer is a frightening word, but cancer of the prostate is a very variable illness. Although it sometimes can be quite malignant, often it is slow growing, so that if it is diagnosed early enough it can be treated successfully and even cured.

Prostatic cancer is found primarily in older men. Therefore, as the average life span gets longer, we are seeing more and more of it. While rarely seen in men under forty, by eighty it's fairly common.

Prostate cancer usually starts in a part of the prostate that is away from the urinary tract, so it rarely causes the kinds of early-warning symptoms that would alert you. But it is extremely important to diagnose prostate cancer early. One of my urology consultants told me that more than half the patients he sees with cancer of the prostate have waited until it's inoperable before coming in. Most of them could have been diagnosed much earlier and probably cured if only they had come in for regular rectal exams. Need I say more?

## PROSTATE SURGERY

Prostatic surgery may be needed in the treatment of BPH if the prostate enlargement is causing blockage of the urinary tract. The three most common methods of BPH surgery are *transurethral resection* (TUR), *suprapubic prostatectomy,* and *retropubic prostatectomy.*

In a TUR, or transurethral resection, an instrument is inserted through your urinary passageway back to your prostate and bladder. Some of the enlarged prostate tissue is then cut away to widen the passage through which you urinate. This alleviates the blockage of urine and allows you to urinate more easily. It is the simplest operation and leaves no scar. It requires just three to six days in the hospital and is preferred for most ordinary cases of prostatic hypertrophy.

For very enlarged prostates, either a suprapubic prostatectomy or a retropubic prostatectomy is performed. These operations are both called "open" prostatectomies because they involve abdominal incisions. The suprapubic operation involves approaching the prostate through the bladder, while the retropubic essentially goes under the bladder.

None of these operations are likely to cause interference with your sexual function. Most patients return to having intercourse three to six weeks after surgery.

## A NEW APPROACH FOR TREATING BPH

BPH usually requires surgery only when the prostate has grown to such an extent that there is danger of urination being completely blocked. Many men experience some of the irritating symptoms of BPH for years but luckily never get to the point where surgery is needed. Unfortunately, until very recently there hasn't been any medication to alleviate these symptoms. It was pretty much all or nothing, with surgery the only solution.

Recently, however, a new treatment, *phenoxybenzamine,* given in pill form, has been introduced to alleviate the symptoms of BPH without surgery. Phenoxybenzamine doesn't shrink the size of the prostate, but it relaxes the muscles in the capsule of the gland which contribute to urinary obstruction by squeezing the prostate. Treatment with phenoxybenzamine is reported to alleviate urinary obstruction symptoms for about 70 percent of patients treated.

Phenoxybenzamine is not a solution for men who already need surgery, but it may offer relief of uncomfortable urinary symptoms to a great many men who don't require surgical intervention. There can be side effects, however, ranging from just annoying, such as fatigue or nasal stuffiness, to potentially serious, such as lowered blood pressure. Your own doctor will have to decide whether it's appropriate for you.

## RETROGRADE EJACULATION

When you ejaculate, your prostate ordinarily expels semen into your urethra. Your bladder-neck sphincter muscle closes so that the ejaculation can't flow backward into your bladder. The ejaculation is then forced out the end of your urethra.

This process is affected by a prostatectomy operation,

since all three of the operations we discussed open and widen your bladder neck surgically. This is done to remove the blockage that was causing those uncomfortable urinary symptoms, and to allow the urine to pass. In most patients, the bladder neck remains permanently open and doesn't close after ejaculation. This means that almost all the ejaculation fluid will flow backward into the bladder, instead of being expelled from the penis.

This is called *retrograde ejaculation,* which means simply "ejaculation backward." It doesn't cause any harm, and the ejaculation fluid comes out later, during urination. Retrograde ejaculation doesn't significantly decrease the sensation of orgasm, and many men don't realize that it's happened until some time afterward, when they notice that no fluid was expelled.

Until recently, nothing could be done about retrograde ejaculation. However, one of my urological consultants has told me that an oral medication, phenylpropanolamine, has recently been discovered to improve bladder-neck tone and allow the semen to be expelled from the penis during orgasm in some patients. It would probably be necessary to take this medication on a regular basis in order for it to be effective, and there could be such possible side effects as sedation, dry mouth, or even possibly an increase in blood pressure.

If you are having retrograde ejaculation subsequent to a prostate operation, check with your physician to see if phenylpropanolamine would be indicated for you. Don't be surprised if your doctor is not initially familiar with it, since this relatively new treatment for retrograde ejaculation has not been discussed extensively in the medical literature.

## CANCER SURGERY

Earlier in this chapter we discussed the three types of prostate surgery commonly used for the surgical treatment of benign prostatic hypertrophy. A fourth procedure, known as *perineal prostatectomy*, involves a surgical approach to the prostate through the area between the scrotum and the anus. It provides a direct route to the prostate and allows for effective removal of a malignant tumor. Unfortunately, however, this operation often damages the nerves involved in obtaining an erection.

Some cases of cancer require the removal of the *entire* prostate and its capsule. The perineal approach was often used for this kind of cancer surgery, but it resulted in a 100 percent incidence of impotence following the operation. Even when a retropubic approach was used, the extensive cancer surgery damaged the nerves responsible for erection.

Recently, however, Dr. Patrick Walsh, a urologist from Johns Hopkins, studied the nerves damaged in cancer surgery to discover why impotence was occurring. In 1983, he and his research team introduced an exciting, modified surgical approach that avoids the nerve centers damaged by the usual cancer surgery. Using this new surgery, erection ability seems to be almost entirely preserved. It is gradually replacing the older surgery, although some doctors are cautious about adopting it, since it will take time to tell for sure whether this technique removes the cancer as completely.

## OTHER TREATMENTS FOR PROSTATE CANCER

One of the basic principles in treating cancer of the prostate is to reduce the amount of testosterone that the body produces, since testosterone may stimulate the cancer. This is sometimes accomplished by giving small amounts of female hormone, which then suppresses testosterone production. In other cases, testosterone is reduced by surgically removing both testicles from the scrotum.

Radiation therapy is an alternative to surgery, but it results in about a 50 percent incidence of impotence. Finally, research is currently focusing on a search for possible chemotherapy for prostate cancer.

The best treatment for prostate cancer—and the one most likely to spare sexual function—is, of course, treatment performed early in the course of the disease. It's therefore important to have any urinary problems diagnosed early and to have regular rectal exams if you're over forty—probably yearly exams if you're over fifty.

## CONTINUING YOUR SEXUAL LIFE AFTER PROSTATE SURGERY

If surgical treatment for cancer of the prostate causes you loss of potency, this doesn't have to mean the end of your sexual life. In Chapter 26 we will describe the use of penile implants. An implant will allow you to have an erection and to continue to enjoy lovemaking even if you've lost your erection ability due to surgery.

There is really no reason for prostate problems to end your sexual life. Even if surgery is involved, chances are great that you will retain your erection ability. But if you do not, an implant will still allow you and your partner to enjoy lovemaking indefinitely.

# 23

# Will a Hysterectomy Affect Your Sexual Life?

It's estimated that more than half of all women in the United States will have a hysterectomy by age sixty-five. It's probably the most common major operation performed in the United States. Theoretically, a hysterectomy should have little or no effect on a woman's sexual life—but unfortunately for some, it does cause major problems.

You might expect that information about the sexual side-effects of hysterectomy would be clear-cut and readily available, but this isn't the case. There is a lot of controversy, and experts on the subject frequently contradict each other. What follows is the best understanding I can give you. It's based on my evaluation of many often-conflicting studies and on my years of clinical practice.

## WHAT IS A HYSTERECTOMY?

Let's start off by defining the terms that we'll be using:
   *Hysterectomy* refers to the removal of your *uterus* (or womb), an organ about the size of a pear that is located at

the end of your vaginal canal. During pregnancy, the fertilized egg attaches itself to the uterine lining, and the fetus
grows inside the uterus. Monthly menstrual periods are the
shedding of the lining of the uterus when it has not been
used for pregnancy.

The part of your uterus that protrudes into the far end
of your vagina is called your *cervix.* The cervix is removed
along with the rest of your uterus during a *complete hysterectomy.*

A hysterectomy will end your menstrual periods if
you're still having them, since menstrual bleeding comes
from your uterus. It will also mean that you can no longer
get pregnant. Your *ovaries,* however, will continue to produce
hormones in a cyclical fashion. When that comes to a stop,
you go through *menopause.*

Sometimes, during a hysterectomy, the ovaries are
removed as well. Removal of your ovaries is called an *oophorectomy.* It produces a "surgical menopause" if you have not
already been through menopause anyway. That's because
the removal of the source of estrogen causes a sudden, sharp
drop in hormonal levels in your body. This may cause such
marked withdrawal symptoms as hot flashes, anxiety, and
irritability. Estrogen replacement therapy is usually advised.

Hysterectomy is customarily performed in one of two
ways. In a *vaginal hysterectomy* the surgery is performed
through the vagina and leaves no external scar. An *abdominal
hysterectomy* is usually performed with a "bikini incision" in
the abdomen just above the pubic area.

The vaginal approach is preferable, because there's a
quicker recovery. However, an abdominal approach is usually necessary if the ovaries have to be removed, if there is
a large tumor or cyst, or if postmenopausal lack of estrogen
has caused vaginal shrinkage. A hysterectomy usually requires about one week in the hospital and one month con-
valescing before you return to full activity.

It's important to keep in mind that the sexual and reproductive organs and functions aren't the same, although they sometimes work together. A hysterectomy removes your uterus, which is primarily a reproductive organ. It doesn't affect your vagina, your clitoris, or your labia, which are your primary sexual organs.

## WHY ARE HYSTERECTOMIES PERFORMED?

Some common causes of hysterectomy for premenopausal women include irregular uterine bleeding or prolonged periods, endometriosis, uterine myomas, and pelvic inflammatory disease.

Older women are more likely to require hysterectomy for postmenopausal bleeding or for cancerous or precancerous conditions of the uterus.

Uterine *prolapse,* or sagging into the vagina, is a common cause for hysterectomy in women of any age who have had several children.

## WILL I LOSE MY FEMININITY?

There are some terrifying myths regarding the after-effects of a hysterectomy. They may leave a woman facing a hysterectomy with unreasonable worries about what will happen to her after the operation, in addition to the anxiety that normally precedes any surgery.

Many of these fears are based on misconceptions about what a hysterectomy actually involves. Louise D., whom I recently treated, became very depressed after surgery and felt that she was "cleaned out and empty inside," that she had somehow lost her femininity and desirability. Other women worry that they will suddenly become overweight or prematurely aged.

Many apprehensions about hysterectomy are, of course, specifically related to a woman's sexual life. She may worry that hysterectomy will end her sexual life entirely, or else cause her to lose her attractiveness, her sexual desire, or her ability to satisfy her partner sexually.

Let's examine the facts. When you're aware of the relatively small size of your nonpregnant uterus, it will be clear to you that you won't be "empty" after a hysterectomy. There is no medical reason for you to suddenly gain weight or to lose your attractiveness. A hysterectomy doesn't end your sexual life. It should have no effect at all on your ability to satisfy your partner sexually, and in most cases it won't have any effect on your sexual desire.

## WHAT CAN I ACTUALLY EXPECT AFTER A HYSTERECTOMY?

There is a wide range of medical opinions about the effects of a hysterectomy. At one end of the spectrum, authorities claim that a hysterectomy should not cause any emotional or sexual problems at all. At the other extreme, studies report that one-third of all women who have undergone the operation suffer a "posthysterectomy syndrome," with depression and loss of sexual desire for several months afterwards.

Actually, reports of the posthysterectomy syndrome's depression and loss of sexual desire seem greatly exaggerated. A few weeks of fatigue and emotionality, which may follow any major stress or surgery, are not abnormal after hysterectomy. However, most studies show women to have improved mood and energy, as well as unimpaired sexual desire and sexual response, when they are evaluated several months after the operation.

One study that examined women both before and after their hysterectomy, for example, reported that 90 percent described themselves as pleased, and 85 percent would encourage a friend to have the procedure performed. Only 4 percent said that they felt worse. Those women who were depressed following the operation generally turned out to have been depressed before as well.

Expectations before a hysterectomy are a very important factor in how you'll feel after it. If you believe that you will lose your femininity, that your partner will no longer desire you, or that you'll lose your own sexual desire, you're more likely to become depressed and to have actual sexual difficulty after the operation. On the other hand, if you look forward to the operation as a way of getting rid of uncomfortable symptoms such as bleeding, urinary incontinence, or painful intercourse, you are likely to feel pleased after the operation and to have undiminished sexual desire.

If your cultural or religious background stresses that pregnancy is the only legitimate reason for sex and that nonfertile women are therefore not considered sexual, you may be more likely to have sexual difficulty. If you strongly desire more children, if you have had depressions before in response to stress, or if you have had many recurrent or chronic physical complaints, you may possibly have trouble after the operation. Even if you are an over-forty woman who had no plans at all of having any more children, you may feel a special sense of loss at the finality of hysterectomy if part of your concept of what makes you feminine is caught up with being a mother and having babies.

The support and encouragement of your partner is very important. Reassurance that he continues to find you sexual and appealing after your hysterectomy will go a long way toward making your response a positive one. If you do continue to feel depressed after a hysterectomy, be sure to get the necessary psychiatric care. It can make a tremendous difference.

## WILL MY SEXUAL LIFE CONTINUE?

Almost all women who were sexually active before a hysterectomy continue to be sexually active afterward. At least 80 percent restart sexual relations within eight weeks following surgery, although more than half feel some mild discomfort at first.

## HOW SHOULD I RESTART INTERCOURSE?

Your gynecologist will probably want to see you about one month after the operation. At this time, he or she will check the back of your vagina to make sure it's completely healed and give you the okay to begin lovemaking.

It's natural to have some apprehension and soreness when you first make love following surgery. Your apprehension can cause lack of vaginal lubrication at first and even some involuntary flinching or constriction of your vaginal opening.

Remember that your clitoris and labia were not affected by the surgery. They shouldn't be tender and you should enjoy clitoral stimulation. Because anxiety can cause lack of lubrication, it's best to use a sexual lubricant at first.

Your partner can help you get used to sex again in a gradual way. Suggest to him that you would like him to stimulate your clitoris, manually or orally. This will help you to get your own natural lubrication back and will help to restore your sexual confidence. Then tell him that you would like to guide first his finger and then his penis into your vagina in a controlled way, and ask that he not do any thrusting until you're sure that you feel comfortable.

You might start with the female superior position, in which you kneel over your partner's hips. You'll feel more in control and more secure in this position. Begin by inserting your partner's penis just partway into your vagina. As you become reassured that it's not painful, you will start to enjoy the feeling of his penis in your vagina again. You can then choose when to continue to full intercourse. If discomfort continues in spite of your precautions, consult with your gynecologist about it.

## WHAT ABOUT THE PROBLEM OF "DRY VAGINA"?

Some women report lack of vaginal lubrication following a hysterectomy. This should be a temporary problem if it's due to anxiety and apprehension. But, if your hysterectomy included the removal of your ovaries, the loss of estrogens can cause a lasting lack of lubrication.

Using a sexual lubricant or lovemaking oil is a simple solution. Estrogen replacement therapy will also help to rapidly restore your vaginal lubrication and to maintain the health of your vaginal tissue.

## WHAT EFFECT WILL THERE BE ON MY SEXUAL DESIRE?

Most women—probably 75 percent of them—find that their level of sexual desire is unaffected by a hysterectomy. Perhaps 20 percent report that they have *more* sexual desire after the hysterectomy—probably because sexual discomfort or other gynecologic symptoms were eliminated by the surgery.

On the other hand, a small minority of women definitely report some decrease of sexual desire. The few I've seen with this problem all had had their ovaries removed as well as their uterus.

Theoretically, this drop in sexual desire shouldn't occur. The androgen hormones that regulate sexual desire are produced primarily by the adrenals in women and shouldn't be affected by removing either the uterus or the ovaries. However, most of women's testosterone, which is the most active androgen, is produced by the ovaries. Removal of the ovaries may thus cause a fall in testosterone levels, and this may produce a loss of sexual desire.

Administering testosterone to a woman who has experienced loss of sexual desire following a hysterectomy and oophorectomy will very likely restore her desire. Estrogen alone can restore vaginal lubrication and prevent atrophy, but it has little or no effect on reestablishing sexual desire. It has therefore been suggested that estrogen replacement therapy for postmenopausal and posthysterectomy women should regularly include a small amount of testosterone to maintain a feeling of well-being and sexual desire. Even if a woman can't take estrogens for medical reasons, she may be able to take testosterone safely.

## WILL I ENJOY INTERCOURSE?
## WILL I BE ABLE TO CLIMAX?

Many women report that they find intercourse more enjoyable after a hysterectomy—especially if they were having physical discomfort before the operation. Many more women find their level of enjoyment essentially unchanged, while only a very few, perhaps 5 percent or less, report diminished enjoyment.

A small but definite group of women report a distinct change in the character of their orgasm, or difficulty in achieving orgasm, after a hysterectomy. Why this should be so is not immediately obvious, since for most women the stimulus for orgasm is either the clitoris or a vaginal trigger-point such as the G-spot. These areas are usually not affected by the operation.

For those women who develop difficulty postoperatively, however, the orgasm was apparently triggered by the thrusting of their partner's penis against their cervix and uterus. They experienced orgasm deep within their pelvis, and may now have considerable difficulty achieving orgasm following a hysterectomy, since the cervix and uterus have been removed. It may be necessary for such a woman to learn to climax with clitoral stimulation. This is not necessarily an unpleasant prospect, but it will require some re-thinking and relearning and an acceptance that her responses are now different.

## WILL A HYSTERECTOMY CAUSE ME TO ENTER MENOPAUSE?

If you've not yet begun menopause, the removal of your ovaries will cause you to enter menopause immediately. Even if your ovaries are left behind, however, a hysterectomy may precipitate an early menopause. This occurs within one to two years after surgery for some women. The reason this happens is not clear, but if it does occur you should consider estrogen replacement therapy.

# PART IV

# OVERCOMING ERECTION DIFFICULTIES

# 24

# Questions You Can Ask Yourself About Your Erection Problems

I have already discussed how a man experiences an inevitable slowdown in his sexual drive and his sexual ability as he ages. It's a rare man who continues, at age fifty-five or sixty, to have the same sexual appetite that he had when he was twenty or twenty-five. But in spite of these changes, your sexual life can actually become more satisfying as you develop more sexual skills, more appreciation of your own sensuality and that of your partner, and more feeling of sexual contentment.

Unfortunately, not every older man experiences this increased enjoyment. For many older men, the slowdown becomes a stop. Erections may become infrequent, too soft for penetration, or nonexistent.

This can be one of the most humiliating experiences an older man may have to endure. Most men don't know where to go for help, and they are often too embarrassed to ask for it anyway. Many men have related to me how their own doctors told them either that there was nothing that could be done at their age, or that the only thing that could help them was a penile implant. While these men felt crushed because they didn't want to give up their sexual life, they also didn't want to consider surgery as a first alternative either.

It's not necessary to give up on your sexual life, and surgery isn't the only alternative. Let me tell you how I would evaluate you at the Sexual Therapy Clinic of San Antonio if you came to me with an erection problem.

## ERECTION DIFFICULTY IS
## A VERY COMMON PROBLEM

I see many, many men with concerns about erection ability, and each case presents a number of possibilities that I have to investigate. Some men suffer from impotence due to med-ical illness, vascular insufficiency, hormonal deficiencies, or medication side-effects. Others have erection difficulty due to anxiety about their functioning, pressure from their part-ner, stress, or relationship difficulties. Still others have no real erection problems at all, but are frightened by some of the normal sexual changes that come with aging.

Emotional and physical factors often interact to add to a man's difficulty. If he is experiencing minor changes in his sexual responses—due to vascular insufficiency, for instance —and he becomes frightened by them, his anxiety can cause him to have much more trouble getting hard than he would have had otherwise. Anxiety about performance can thus magnify the sexual difficulty that a medical condition may be causing.

Over the years, I have compiled a list of questions that help me to assess whether a patient's erection problems are primarily medical or emotional. They also give me some clues as to what the specific problem is. You can ask yourself the same questions before going to your personal physician.

The answers you get will give you at least a preliminary idea of what's wrong. In addition, not every doctor you may consult may know very much about sexual problems, so your own preliminary evaluation may help you to judge whether the physician has a reasonable grasp of the problem.

## DO YOU NOT GET ERECTIONS AT ALL, OR DO YOU GET THEM BUT THEN LOSE THEM?

This seems like a simple question but my interpretation of your answer depends in part on my experience in treating hundreds of men with these problems.

If, for example, you tell me that a few years ago you gradually began to lose your erections more and more easily and that now you don't get any erections at all, chances are you have a slowly developing physical problem. If you get erections that are terrific until you try to penetrate but then rapidly go down just as you enter your partner, your problem is probably due to anxiety about your performance. If your erection comes up halfway or three-quarters with a lot of stimulation but then goes right back down as soon as the stimulation ends, it's more likely to be a physical problem. If your erection comes up normally but then fades during intercourse, it could mean that the valves in your penile veins are letting the blood leak out of your erection and back into your general body circulation. If, on the other hand, you are able to have intercourse for a good while, perhaps ten or fifteen minutes, but then your erection sometimes fades away, there's probably nothing wrong with you at all. One erection doesn't have to stay forever. If it goes down, your partner can probably help you get it back. If you don't climax on a particular occasion, it probably just means that your body doesn't need a climax at that time.

## DO YOU OCCASIONALLY
## AWAKEN WITH A FIRM ERECTION?

This is a good way to tell whether your erectile mechanism has the capacity to function. If it does, you will, during the course of an ordinary night's sleep, have three or four erections lasting approximately twenty minutes each. These occur during the stage of sleep called REM sleep, or dream sleep. You may not be aware of the erections while you're asleep, but if you happen to awaken during this stage of sleep you will be likely to awaken with an erection.

If you awaken with a full bladder, that's not the cause of the erection. It's just that your urge to urinate happened to wake you up during a dream-sleep stage.

If you do notice fairly regular middle-of-the-night or morning erections, it's a good indication that your erection mechanism is intact and does have the capacity to function. If you are aware of erections on awakening only very infrequently or not at all, or else if they are very soft erections, it doesn't necessarily prove that your erection mechanism isn't working—you just may not be waking up during the appropriate stage of sleep—but it certainly does raise suspicions that your erection mechanism may be impaired.

## CAN YOU GET ERECT IN SOME
## SITUATIONS BUT NOT IN OTHERS?

This is a good way to tell whether your erection difficulty is due to the particular circumstances of your lovemaking or if there's a medical problem. For example, having difficulty getting erect when you're very fatigued or under a lot of emotional stress is fairly normal. If, on the other hand, you have problems getting erect with one partner but not another, it may be due to tension that you're feeling in one of the relationships, or it may be that with one partner you feel secure but with the other you feel a lot of pressure to perform. It may even be that one partner helps you get hard and the other doesn't. If erection difficulties occur only with new partners, it's probably because you feel anxiety about your sexual performance in these situations. If you can get erections when you're away on vacation but have difficulty when you're at home, your difficulty may be due to work-related stress.

## DOES YOUR PARTNER HELP BY STIMULATING YOUR PENIS? DOES IT WORK WHEN SHE DOES?

This is really an important question. If you're not getting help from your partner, it may turn out that there is nothing wrong with you at all. As you get older, you are simply not going to be getting spontaneous erections the way you did when you were younger. You require some direct physical stimulation to your penis in order to get hard. If your partner isn't helping you because she doesn't realize your need for it or because she has leftover inhibitions about touching your penis, your trouble may be due simply to lack of stimulation.

If you are able to get good erections when your partner is stimulating you, there is nothing wrong with your erection mechanism at all. There's nothing unusual or abnormal about requiring stimulation. You and your partner may simply need to take more time for caressing and foreplay before attempting intercourse.

On the other hand, if you don't get erect even with adequate stimulation, either a medical condition could be causing the problem, or intense performance anxiety could be blocking your natural sexual response.

## CAN YOU GET ERECT
## WITH MASTURBATION?

If you can get firm erections with masturbation, your sexual response system is intact. Masturbation when you're alone allows you to try out your erection mechanism in a situation with less anxiety about performance and less embarrassment.

If you have difficulty getting erect during lovemaking, even with some stimulation, but you can get erect with masturbation, there are two possibilities. One is that anxieties about getting hard, or other emotional feelings such as anger or resentment, are blocking your sexual response. The other possibility is that your partner isn't giving you the kind of sexual stimulation that you need. This could be because you've never told her what you'd like or shown her explicitly how to do it. Talking about it might be a little embarrassing, but it can really help.

## DID YOUR ERECTION DIFFICULTY
## START WITH A PARTICULAR,
## EMOTIONALLY UPSETTING EXPERIENCE?

If your problem started around the time of a divorce or separation, the loss of a job, your retirement, a period of financial stress, the death of your spouse, rejection by your partner, or any similar stressful situation, your erection difficulty was probably a natural response to stress. It may, however, have caused you worry about your erection ability. If your erection problem has continued past the stress period, it could be that this performance anxiety has continued to interfere.

## HOW DO YOU REACT IF YOU HAVE TROUBLE GETTING HARD? HOW DOES YOUR PARTNER REACT?

If you tell me your partner becomes angry, accusing, or tearful if you don't get erect, I must suspect that you feel very pressured to perform. If you become angry or disgusted with yourself if things go wrong, you put the same pressure on yourself.

On the other hand, if your partner is supportive and helpful and you yourself are philosophical but, *even so,* you have trouble getting hard, there would seem to be less likelihood of your erection difficulty being caused by anxiety alone, and a greater possibility that medical factors might be to blame.

## ARE YOU TAKING MEDICINE THAT COULD CAUSE ERECTION DIFFICULTIES?

As discussed in chapters 19 and 20, many medications can cause erection difficulties. The most prominent of these are the antihypertensives, but many other types of medicines, both mentioned and not included in this book, occasionally cause problems. Review any medicine you might be taking, and check with your own physician if you've a question.

Remember, if you are taking a medication that has been known to occasionally cause sexual difficulties this doesn't necessarily prove that that medication is the cause of *your* problem. There are many other possible causes for erection difficulties.

# 25

# How We Evaluate and Treat Impotence

If you have erection problems, I hope that you've already asked yourself the questions posed in the previous chapter. If so, by now you may have some idea of the possible causes of your difficulty. Keep in mind, though, that a comprehensive medical evaluation is necessary to more accurately pin down the exact problem and to define a treatment plan. Unfortunately, very few places can provide this kind of evaluation. In this chapter I will describe how we use a comprehensive evaluation and treatment program at the Sexual Therapy Clinic of San Antonio.

The diagnosis and treatment of impotence has made remarkable strides in recent years. At one time, scientists were reluctant to become involved in sexual research. Now medical science and technology are working on overcoming erection problems just as they would with any other medical condition.

Not too many years ago, impotence was thought to be psychologically caused in almost all cases, because we simply didn't have the means of medically evaluating the problem. The first step toward a fuller understanding came when tests were developed to help distinguish between medical and psychological causes. Then a radical new development was introduced: penile implants to surgically treat impotent men. Soon the pendulum swung the other way. Men with impotence were no longer told that it was all in their heads. Instead, they were being told that surgery was their only hope.

Progress has continued in the past few years. Developments in medical pharmacology and technology have provided a wide spectrum of investigative tools and treatment methods to help men with impotence.

Unfortunately, many who claim to treat impotence are still years behind. Some nonmedical "sexual therapists" still attempt to treat impotent men with sexual counseling alone —ignoring all we have learned in recent years about the medical causes of the problem. Others, like some physicians, still think only in terms of implant surgery for every impotent man. This is also completely unwarranted. Penile implants work extremely well when they are needed, but there are now many other means of treatment that don't require surgery. Automatically recommending surgery without seeing whether a man's erectile mechanism can be improved by simple medical means is outmoded and unjustified.

## HOW AN EVALUATION OF YOUR ERECTION PROBLEM BEGINS AT THE SEXUAL THERAPY CLINIC

As mentioned in the last chapter, my first step is to try to get a clear idea of the exact nature of your erection problem. I ask how long you've had the problem and how it developed; whether you can't get erections at all or whether you get them at first but then can't maintain them; whether you can associate the start of your erection difficulty with any specific emotional incident in your life, with a medical problem, or with starting a medication. I try to get an idea about your relationship with your partner and how she reacts if you have difficulty.

It's important to determine whether you actually do have an impotence problem. Men sometimes come to me with fears of impotence when the real problem is just a lack of understanding about some of the natural physiological changes of aging.

If, for example, a man having difficulty is also not getting adequate stimulation from his partner, the problem can often be rectified with a bit of education. In cases like this, explaining to a man and his partner that his penis now needs help in order to get erect and teaching the woman how to give that help may be all that's needed to improve the man's sexual functioning.

## IS IT A PHYSICAL PROBLEM OR A PSYCHOLOGICAL ONE?

As mentioned earlier, I get clues as to whether your problem is psychological or physical, and whether your erection mechanism is actually intact, from your ability to get erections with masturbation and/or whether you awaken with erections.

If you can tell me that you wake up several mornings a week with a good, hard erection, I *know* that you are getting good nocturnal erections. Further tests to demonstrate this are unnecessary, a waste of your time and money. If, on the other hand, you are aware of very infrequent nighttime erections, or else have none at all, it may be worthwhile to investigate further.

A rather sophisticated test has been developed to evaluate your nighttime erections. The "nocturnal penile tumescence test" (the NPT test) is simple and painless, but it's rather expensive and inconvenient, as it requires you to spend from one to three nights in a hospital or sleep lab where NPT monitoring can be accomplished.

Because of the expense and inconvenience of the hospital NPT test, simplified machines have been developed that you can take home to use, but the procedure is still fairly expensive. This has spurred a search for simpler, less expensive ways to measure nighttime erections.

One amazingly simple but ingenious variation, the "stamp test," uses a ring of postage stamps placed around the shaft of your penis. If you obtain a full erection, your erection should split the perforations. This test is subject to errors and inexactness, but it's a good first approximation. If you break the stamps three nights out of three, it certainly indicates that your erection mechanism is functional.

Another test, the "snap-gauge," consists of a Velcro band slipped around your penis. It has three tiny plastic threads, and if your penis gets hard enough for vaginal penetration, all three threads theoretically will break.

At the Sexual Therapy Clinic of San Antonio we tend to use tests of nighttime erection only for supplementary evidence. We usually have a good idea whether or not you are awakening with firm erections from your own report. We also know that almost all of our older patients will have at least some physical or vascular component to their erection problem.

When in doubt, we often use the stamp test and sometimes the snap-gauge. We usually use the NPT test itself only as a prelude to surgery when documentation is needed. It's simply not required at earlier stages of treatment, and for all its expense and sophistication, it rarely makes much difference in determining the course of treatment.

All in all, tests of nighttime erections must be interpreted with caution. If you get no nighttime erections, it's usually a good indication that you have a physical problem. However, I'm not sure that getting a reflex erection in your sleep necessarily proves that you should be able to get hard in a sexual situation or that the problem is "in your head."

## COULD A SUBSTANCE
## YOU ARE TAKING BE
## AFFECTING YOUR SEXUAL FUNCTIONING?

The antihypertensive medications are the most likely cul-
prits, but there are many other possibilities. Because your
high blood pressure, if you have it, needs to be treated, we
will search for a medication that will control that problem
without suppressing your sexual functioning. It's the same
with medications you may be taking for other illnesses.

Long-term overuse of alcohol and cigarettes causes
major sexual problems for many of the older men who come
to the clinic. Remember, amounts of alcohol that presented
no problem when you were in your twenties may be enough
to overwhelm your erection reflex now that you are older
and your erections have become more fragile.

Two other substances I've learned to look for in treating
sexual dysfunction are caffeine and nasal sprays. Overuse of
caffeine can cause a great deal of anxiety, which can interfere
with erection. With regard to nasal decongestant sprays, I
know of two impotent men who started with them originally
for sinus conditions but continued habitual use four to five
times a day for years. The blood-vessel constrictors in the
spray were being absorbed into the general circulation and
interfering with erection. The impotence problems substan-
tially cleared when the men stopped using the sprays.

## COULD AN ILLNESS BE
## AFFECTING YOU SEXUALLY?

I especially look for arteriosclerosis, high blood pressure,
diabetes, hormonal problems, or chronic liver or kidney dysfunction.

Diabetes stands out as a frequent cause of erection
problems. Many men who have had this disease for some
time develop a decreased erection ability, either because of

neuropathy (nerve damage) or because of vascular damage (partial blockage of the blood supply to the penis). Some men we see for erection difficulties don't realize that they have diabetes, while others have known about it for years but often have not taken good care of themselves.

Arteriosclerosis, or hardening of the arteries, causes blockage of the small blood vessels leading to the penis the same way that it blocks the blood flow in other parts of the body. Chronic liver disease can cause alteration in the ways that sexual hormones are metabolized in the body and result in a relative lack of male hormones.

Hypothyroidism (low thyroid hormone) can also be associated with decreased production and increased breakdown of male hormones. Patients with this condition may have increased production of prolactin, a pituitary hormone that suppresses sexual desire and erection in men. Patients with hypothyroidism may also develop fatigue, lethargy, or depression, all of which may also suppress sexual desire and functioning.

We test for these conditions in a number of ways. Laboratory evaluations can be especially helpful. A chemistry profile gives us a blood sugar level to screen for diabetes and also tests various liver and kidney functions. In most cases, we also check thyroid function.

A further word about the hormone prolactin, whose elevated levels can cause sexual difficulty: Produced by the pituitary gland, its primary function is to stimulate women's breasts to produce milk. While also produced in small quantities in men, it doesn't have any male function that we know of, but if too much of it is produced, depression of male sexual desire, suppression of testosterone production, and erection difficulty may result.

Various conditions can elevate prolactin levels. One is the presence of a pituitary adenoma, a small, usually nonmalignant tumor, which produces very high levels of this hormone. Other conditions that can cause moderate elevations are hypothyroidism and various medications, such as major tranquilizers. Stress can also contribute. For this reason, most impotent men coming to the clinic are checked for prolactin elevation.

In chapter 2, I discussed at length the role of testosterone, your primary male hormone, in sexual function. As this hormone may be depressed in many older men, we also check its levels as part of our workup.

## THE UROLOGICAL EXAM

If one of our urologists examines you for impotence, he'll check your testicles for signs of atrophy or shrinkage that could indicate inadequate testicular function. A rectal exam will enable him to check your prostate gland for signs of enlargement, infection, or tumor.

Your penis will be examined for any abnormality and especially for signs of Peyronies disease. This peculiar condition, seen more commonly in older men, results in a fibrous thickening or plaque on the side or top of the penis, which can cause sharp bending of the penis with erection. This can be quite painful. The condition can also create an inability to get erect. Its cause is unknown.

An important part of the urological examination will be a test of your perineal sensation and bulbocaverosal reflex to make sure that the nerve supply that produces erections is not grossly impaired.

The urologist will also perform a simple test of the blood pressure in your penis and will compare the results with the blood pressure in the rest of your body to help us estimate whether the circulation to your penis has been impaired by arteriosclerosis or other conditions. As with so many other tests dealing with impotence, this one isn't 100 percent certain either. Some men with good blood pressure in their penises still can't get erect, while other men with what seems to be decreased penile blood pressure get fine erections.

When men come to us with erection problems, they occasionally tell us how previous urologists have done huge workups, which have included IVPs and cystoscopies. In almost all cases, an IVP (kidney evaluation) and cystoscopy (bladder evaluation) are irrelevant in an impotence workup; there's no reason for you to go through the unnecessary expense and inconvenience of these tests.

## IF THE PROBLEM IS DUE TO LACK OF STIMULATION OR ANXIETY ABOUT PERFORMANCE

As I mentioned earlier, one of the easiest problems to treat is simple lack of penile stimulation. Educating the two of you together makes for the most effective treatment. Both of you need to realize that an older man usually requires assistance from his partner to get erect. It's time to set aside your inhibitions about a woman touching a man's penis if you want to continue to have a satisfying sexual life together.

If worry about how you're going to perform sexually is complicating your erection difficulty, we would try to work with you and your regular partner, if you have one. If you do not, or if she is unwilling to cooperate, we will work with you alone. Among other suggestions, we often recommend "sensate focus" exercises for you to use at home in private. Their aim is to remove some of the pressure for performance that you are feeling and enable you to get your confidence back and thus to improve your sexual function.

We also frequently prescribe various medications that may make it easier for you to get erect and thus help give you more confidence.

Then there are erection-aid devices, which can help you achieve and maintain an erection. Most of them work on a vacuum principle and pull blood into your penis to help you get hard. These devices are simple, relatively inexpensive, externally applied, and don't require any surgery. They seem to be safe, if used sensibly and according to instruction. If you're having a great deal of anxiety, we may give you one of these erection-aid devices to fall back on to produce an erection if you don't get one on your own. This can be a tremendous help in alleviating your anxiety. Just knowing you have it in reserve may help you to relax enough to get your confidence back and resume getting erections on your own.

Your partner may well have become frustrated with your erection difficulties, which is certainly understandable, but her frustration can mean additional pressure for you. We will explain to her how getting upset and criticizing you actually gets her a result opposite to the one she wants.

If part of your difficulty is due to fatigue or stress, we would work with you on changing some of the environmental factors in your life. We would also suggest such simple alterations as making love in the morning, when you're relaxed and not under pressure.

## IF THERE ARE MEDICATION SIDE-EFFECTS

As you know by now, quite a number of frequently used medications can cause loss of sexual desire and loss of erection ability. Because their sexual side-effects are not widely publicized, your physician may not be aware of them.

If we discover that you may be taking one or more medications that could be contributing to your sexual difficulties, we would try to advise you of simple alternatives that have less risk of causing such effects. In some cases, we would consult with one of our own consultants to determine the best alternative medication for you. We would then work in conjunction with your own physician to formulate the best treatment plan for you.

Often we may not be sure that a specific medication is adversely affecting your sexual function. In that case, we may suggest strategies to test whether this medication or some other factor is the primary cause.

As we mentioned earlier, excessive alcohol use and cigarette smoking are very common causes of erection difficulty, especially in older men. If either of these circumstances is contributing in a major way to your sexual difficulties, we would strongly urge that you make some alterations in your consumption patterns. We find that it's relatively easy for men to cut back on their alcohol consumption when they realize that it is causing sexual difficulties. Cigarette smoking, on the other hand, is a very difficult addiction to break, sometimes even in the face of impotence. Some men are able to overcome it, but for others it's necessary to work around the habit and still try to help them restore their sexual function.

## IF THERE IS A MEDICAL OR PHYSICAL CAUSE

The first step is, of course, to try and get any illness under control. We sometimes see men with diabetes, for instance, whose diabetes is completely out of control. No one is going to be able to get good erections with a blood-sugar level of 400. Similarly, if a man has hypothyroidism, it's readily treatable. Excess prolactin can often be treated very simply by medication, as well.

But what if your problem is due to a chronic condition, such as arteriosclerosis or long-standing diabetes or hypertension? Not too many years ago, if you had erection difficulties due to a medical illness such as this, it was thought that the only treatment available to you was surgery and a penile implant. Things have changed tremendously since then. Many types of treatments can be tried before implant surgery is considered, beginning with oral medications and moving on to erection-aid devices and injections of medication into the penis.

Recently, a number of oral medications have been found to have value in overcoming erection problems. They are not aphrodisiacs in the classical sense of giving you more sexual desire; rather, they can improve the ease with which you can get an erection, increase its firmness, and improve your ability to maintain it. Some of these medications work by improving the circulation in and blood supply to the penis. The mechanisms of others are not known.

Oral medications may be helpful in perhaps a third to a half of impotent patients. They don't work on an all-or-nothing basis, but they can cause at least partial improvements in sexual functioning when they are successful. A man who has soft, poorly maintained erections may experience a 30 percent improvement with medication. This may be enough to make his erections quite adequate for intercourse. Another man who has little or no erection activity to start with might not experience enough improvement from the medications to notice. On the other hand, there might be enough partial improvement for him to be able to have intercourse on occasion with a semierect or three-quarter-erect penis—which still might be an only partially acceptable solution—or he might experience a return of full erections.

Another medication treatment, discussed earlier, involves the use of testosterone. If your levels of this hormone are deficient, receiving injections of it monthly or biweekly may be extremely helpful, especially in conjunction with one or more of the other medicines.

## AND IF THE MEDICATIONS DON'T WORK?

As mentioned before, if medication therapy doesn't help, several different kinds of **erection-aid devices** are available. While these devices will produce erections for most men, not every patient is happy with them. Some people find them uncomfortable to use. Somewhat bulky, they are not the kind of thing you would slip into your jacket pocket. This makes them most suitable for a man in a long-standing stable relationship with an understanding partner. For someone who is divorced, widowed, or single and dating a number of different women, such an aid may not be practical.

If an erection-aid device proves unsatisfactory, you might consider **penile injections**. This relatively new treatment involves the injection of small amounts of blood-vessel dilators directly into the corpora cavernosa of your penis with a very fine needle. In most cases these injections produce an almost immediate erection that lasts about an hour. You can learn how to administer the injections at home yourself. This treatment is probably successful in 85 to 90 percent of cases.

Unfortunately, there are some drawbacks. The first is the very fact of injections into the penis—an act some men find painful to even contemplate. There can also be some potentially serious immediate side-effects, such as an erection that won't go down and requires emergency treatment. While this is unlikely, it can occur, as can other reactions to the medication. Since this treatment is still fairly new, there may well be long-term side effects that we're not yet aware of but that may result from repeated injections into the penis. We also don't know how long a treatment like this will continue to work, or whether, over a period of years, the injections will lose their effectiveness.

Another newly developing area of treatment for impotence is **surgery on the vascular system** of the penis. There are two different types of such surgery. The first bypasses obstructions in the blood supply to the penis, much like a cardiac bypass operation. Unfortunately, though, the blood vessels are smaller, the surgery more difficult, and the results less successful than with cardiac bypasses.

While the first type of surgery is meant to increase the amount of blood going into the penis through the arteries to produce an erection, the second type tries to keep erections by decreasing the amount of blood leaving the penis through the veins. Some men cannot get or maintain an erection because the blood leaks out of their penis too readily in what are called corporal venous leaks. In this surgery the offending veins are tied off. Again, the results of this surgery are not 100 percent.

Although penile vascular surgery is becoming the subject of more and more research, only a few centers such as ours, where urologic surgeons are experienced and specially trained, currently offer it. Expensive penile arteriograms and other studies of your penile circulation are not warranted as part of an impotence evaluation unless vascular surgery is seriously contemplated.

Most men who don't respond to other treatment to overcome their impotence are recommended for a surgical **implant**. Penile implant operations are quite common, safe, and successful. And they work! They are an excellent alternative for a man who wants to maintain his erection ability but has not responded to, or chooses not to use, the other means of treatment outlined here. I'll tell you more about implants in the next chapter.

Men sometimes come to me feeling hopeless because they haven't been able to have intercourse for four or five years or more. With the progress that medical science has made in the past few years, I can truly say that it doesn't matter how long it's been since you've been able to get erections. With the wide array of treatments available in a comprehensive treatment program such as ours, there's a great likelihood that some method will be capable of restoring your sexual functioning.

# 26

# The Penile Implant: What It Is and How It Works

The previous chapter included the wide range of nonsurgical treatments currently available for men with impotence, as well as new surgical treatments now being developed. Unfortunately, nonsurgical treatments are not always successful, and the new surgical treatments are neither widely available nor universally effective. However, there is a treatment, well tested and widely used, that can enable you to have erections again, at any age, no matter what the cause of your impotence: the penile implant.

My patients tend to have many questions about penile implants. Some men arrive knowing that a penile implant is what they want. Others, on the other hand, are certain they don't want surgery under any circumstances. Many men, not really sure what a penile implant actually is, tend to think in terms of what they've read about heart transplants, for instance, or artificial limbs.

A penile implant *is not* an artificial penis that replaces your own. It's not a transplant like a heart transplant or a corneal transplant. A penile implant is simply a replacement of the *erection mechanism* of your penis.

The implant, consisting of two silicone-covered cylinders, is surgically inserted into your penis much the way a
breast implant is placed within a woman's breast in an enlargement operation. Just as the breast implant leaves the
external appearance of the breast unchanged except for the
increase in size, a penile implant inside your penis doesn't
appreciably alter its outward appearance. If you could have
climaxes and ejaculate before you had the implant, you
should be able to do so afterward. You can even father a
child.

## HOW YOUR ERECTION
## MECHANISM NORMALLY WORKS

Under normal circumstances, you get an erection when
blood fills two long, spongy cylinders, the corpora cavernosa, that run the length of your penis. The blood is held in
these cylinders by thousands of tiny valves. Your erection
becomes firm and hard much the same way that a long,
cylindrical balloon becomes stiff when you inflate it. When
the valves release, the extra blood drains from your penis
and the erection deflates.

This erection mechanism can be very fragile, as it requires your vascular and nervous systems to work together
in a complicated fashion. Many different factors can cause
it to work irregularly or not at all. If your erection system
isn't working and it can't be restored by medication or other
nonsurgical means, it can be replaced by penile implants
inserted into your corpora cavernosa.

## THE DIFFERENT KINDS OF IMPLANTS

There are four basic types, the first of which is the **inflatable
penile implant**. *(See Figure 26–1.)* This device very accurately
mimics your normal erection process. Two empty silicone-

**Fig. 26.1** Inflatable penile implant. (Courtesy of American Medical Systems, Inc.)

covered cylindrical balloons are implanted in the corpora cavernosa of your penis. When you want to have an erection, you squeeze a tiny pump implanted in your scrotum. This forces a saline fluid from a reservoir into the expandable balloons in your penis. The fluid causes your penis to extend and expand into a nearly normal erection. *(See Figure 26–2.)*

After using the erection, you can press a little release valve on the pump. The balloons will deflate, the fluid returns to the reservoir, and your penis returns to its limp state. Accidental deflation won't occur unless there's a mechanical breakdown of some kind.

The second type of penile implant is called the **semi-**

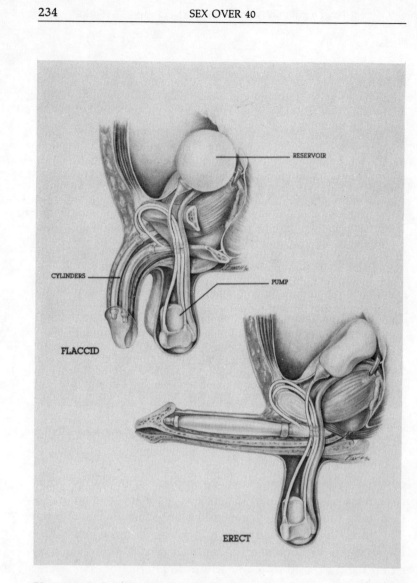

**Fig. 26.2** Inflatable penile implant in flaccid and erect positions. (Courtesy of American Medical Systems, Inc.)

**rigid implant**. *(See Figure 26–3.)* Consisting of solid silicone cylinders, this device has no pump or fluid reservoir, and the penis stays erect all the time.

This semirigid "rod" implant has probably been used more widely than any other, because of its simplicity, surgical ease of implantation, and lower cost. It's major disadvantage, however, is the awkwardness of having a constant erection. The concealment of the bulge can be difficult.

Both of the aforementioned types of implants were introduced at approximately the same time in the early 1970s. Several years later, the **flexible implant** was introduced. This device attempted to keep the advantages of the rod implant, such as simplicity, ease of surgery, and lack of mechanical complexity, while overcoming the problems of having a constant erection and needing to conceal it. It consists of flexible, silicone-covered cylinders surrounding an inner core made of braided silver or stainless steel wire. The wire core allows it to maintain a position until you adjust it again. For instance, you can straighten it into an erect position for intercourse, or bend it down, out of the way, when it's not in use.

In the early 1980s, a fourth type of implant was introduced whose design was meant to retain certain advantages of an inflatable implant while avoiding some of its disadvantages. The **self-contained inflatable rod** implant consists of two saline-filled silicone cylinders, with the pump mechanism and fluid reservoir contained within the rods themselves. *(See Figure 26–4.)* This allows them to be implanted entirely within the penis, the same way the standard semirigid implants are.

Now that we are familiar with the principles on which these devices work, let's examine the advantages and disadvantages of each.

*The three-part inflatable implant.* The inflatable implant consists of two expandable silicone balloons surgically inserted into the erectile tubes of your penis. You don't feel

**Fig. 26.3** Semirigid penile implant. (Courtesy of American Heyer-Schulte Co.)

**Fig. 26.4** Self-contained inflatable rod penile implant. (Courtesy of Surgitek, Medical Engineering Corp.)

them once the surgery heals. They are connected to a small reservoir balloon inserted in the fatty tissue of your abdomen just in front of your bladder. A tiny pump hangs in your scrotum, above your testicles. The implant is cosmetically unnoticable. There is no scar on your penis, since the incision is on your abdomen or scrotum. The penis looks normal in both the erect and flaccid states. There is a potential problem, however, in that you are dealing with a rather complex hydraulic system that is subject to occasional mechanical breakdowns. While these breakdowns aren't serious (a kinked piece of tubing or a fluid leak, for instance), they usually require reoperation to be fixed. About 5 percent of patients will undergo reoperation each year to repair one of these minor mechanical failures. This can be annoying, uncomfortable, and expensive, and there can be some danger, however slight, of surgical complications. Let's review both the pros and cons.

*Advantages:*

1. Your penis looks like a naturally functioning penis, and your erections resemble normal erections. Besides just being erect, your penis actually fills out in width and becomes full. This doesn't happen with the rod implants or the flexible implants and happens only slightly with the inflatable rods.

2. There's no problem with concealment. The erection is flaccid when you're not using it. The implant is relatively undetectable—and comfortable.

*Disadvantages:*

1. It requires more difficult, longer surgery and more skill and experience on the part of the surgeon.

2. Mechanical failures may necessitate reoperation.

3. The costs of both the implant and the surgery are greater than for the semirigid or flexible implants.

*The semirigid rod implant.* Simple and reliable, the mechanism consists of two silicone rods implanted in your penis. The implant itself is much cheaper than is the inflatable. The surgery may involve an incision on your penis or through your scrotum.

*Advantages:*

1. The cost is lower than the inflatable implant.

2. It's simple, not mechanical, and can't break down.

3. The surgery is simple, requires less skill on the surgeon's part, and there's less likelihood of repeat surgery.

*Disadvantages:*

1. Your constant erection can make concealment in street clothes a problem, although a jockstrap or tight undershorts will usually take care of this problem.

2. The rod can cause pain or discomfort, either from your semierect penis rubbing against your clothing all day or from its being strapped out of the way. (Few actually do complain of discomfort, however.)

3. The rods can slowly lose length from being gradually pushed back into the pelvic tissue.

4. If it's poorly fit, the constant pressure of the erection can irritate and even erode surrounding tissue, which could possibly necessitate a reoperation to remove the implant.

5. The tip of the penis may droop slightly, producing a slightly less than normal-looking erection.

6. Some patients feel that the erection, which doesn't fill out in girth, doesn't feel firm enough.

7. With the semirigid implant in place, your doctor may have difficulty doing a cystoscopy or other urologic procedure if you need it.

8. Some "rotational instability" has been reported in a few cases. This means that the rods don't stay exactly where they belong (alongside each other), but one may slide slightly over or under the other.

9. The rod implants can increase urinary resistance, which can be significant if you already have some partial obstruction—from an enlarged prostate, for example.

*The flexible implant.* Self-contained, like the semirigid rod, it can be bent into shape and it will stay in that shape because of its inner core of braided silver wire. This implant is basically a variant of the semirigid, and it has a lot of the same advantages and disadvantages. It has the surgical simplicity and lack of mechanical problems of the rod implants, while avoiding some of the cosmetic problems and inconveniences of your having a constant erection. After a long period of time, the silver wires in the flexible implant may wear out and break from constantly being bent back and forth. The implant then would lose its ability to keep a position it's bent into and would return to the constantly erect position.

*The self-contained inflatable rods.* These silicone-covered cylinders have a pump and reservoir mechanism included within the rod itself. When it's not inflated, your penis hangs down limply, but because the fluid and the mechanism are both inside the rod, your penis doesn't have the total limpness of the empty balloon of the three-part inflatable implant.

When you want to use the inflatable rod, you squeeze a pump on the rod, within or just behind the head of your penis, depending on the model. This forces fluid within the cylinder into a nonexpandable inner cylinder that inflates and becomes firm. Just a segment in the midportion of the inflatable rod, therefore, actually inflates.

Different models have slightly different mechanisms to

deflate them but, depending on the model, pressing a deflation valve near the head, or else bending your penis at the base to expel the fluid from the inflation chamber, returns the organ to its limper state.

In many ways, this type of implant is most comparable to the flexible rods we just discussed rather than to the three-part inflatable implants.

The advantages over the three-part implant include easier surgery and far fewer mechanical breakdowns. The disadvantages: a less natural limpness, less natural erection, and less expansion of girth with erection.

Unlike semirigid rods, these inflatable rods can place the penis into a semilimp position for more comfort and better cosmetic appearance. On the other hand, inflatable rods cost more than the semirigid variety, and certain positions may very rarely cause the implant to deflate in the midst of intercourse.

## WHO USES PENILE IMPLANTS?

Many tens of thousands of inflatable implants have been used successfully, and probably an even larger number of the semirigid rods have been used. Clearly, penile implants are far from experimental.

Approximately three-quarters of the men who have received penile implants are between the ages of forty and seventy. However, men as young as nineteen or twenty have received implants because of erection inability due to accidents or medical illness, and men in their eighties have also received them. About 10 percent of implants are given to men older than seventy years of age.

Men most commonly require penile implants due to impotence from diabetes, vascular disease, certain types of prostate or rectal surgery, pelvic nerve injury, and spinal cord injury.

When penile implants were first introduced, implant

surgery wasn't performed if a patient's erection problems had emotional causes. Now, however, if psychotherapy and sexual therapy have been tried and haven't helped, these patients can also be candidates for penile implants.

## WHAT KIND OF OPERATION IS REQUIRED?

As mentioned before, the most complicated and lengthy surgery is required for the three-part inflatable implant. It will take about an hour and a half to two hours, as opposed to about forty-five minutes to an hour for one of the three types of self-contained rod implants. The incidence of post-operative infection is only about 1.5 percent for all types of implants.

The average hospital stay for a patient recuperating from an inflatable implant is about three days. For a semi-rigid rod implant or one of the other types of rod implants, the stay is usually shorter, and some of the procedures are actually performed on an outpatient surgery basis.

The overall success rate with all kinds of implants is in the range of 95 percent, but this varies depending on the skill and expertise of the individual surgeon involved.

You will probably be told to wait three to six weeks before having intercourse. Most patients do wait close to six weeks. A small number of patients (probably less than 5 percent) have some degree of pain continuing for a time after surgery. In almost all cases, this eventually disappears.

## HOW SATISFIED ARE MEN AND THEIR PARTNERS WITH THE RESULTS?

Reaction seems to be very positive. Most men report good sensation and enjoyable lovemaking with an implant, particularly with the inflatable variety.

A recent article by Dr. Brantley Scott from Baylor College of Medicine included the opinions of a group of men who had received inflatable implants. About 85 percent of them said they were satisfied or very satisfied with their sexual responses. Only one man out of thirty-nine reported full dissatisfaction. All the female partners who responded felt that they would recommend the operation to a couple considering it.

If a man's partner is positive about lovemaking, her response to an implant will probably be very good. Rather than feeling uncomfortable with the idea, most women tend to be quite happy with their partner's new potency. But it's important to have realistic expectations: if your partner is very negative about sex before you have an implant, your having an implant probably won't change her attitude.

Men who were impotent but now have an implant generally experience an improvement in self-esteem, knowing that they can now have sexual relations. Even single men who do little dating and only use their implant infrequently say that just knowing that they are capable of having intercourse is very important to them. They feel more comfortable with women, knowing that if a situation led to a romantic sexual encounter, they would have the capacity to perform.

## IN CONCLUSION

A penile implant can make an enormous difference to a man who has erection problems but doesn't respond to other forms of treatment. If you are one of these men, you have the opportunity to continue an active sex life indefinitely. Aside from your own enjoyment, this can give you the self-esteem of continuing to please your partner, as well as the warmth and intimacy that a continued loving and sexual relationship can bring.

# CONCLUSION

# SEX IN A LONG-TERM RELATIONSHIP

# Recapturing Intensity

Keeping a long-term relationship fresh is a problem all couples face. We seek out long-term relationships for the security and comfort they provide, yet we want our sexual relations to feel new, fresh, and exciting. The question is how we can maintain newness, freshness, and continuing intensity in a sexual relationship that is no longer new.

This dilemma does not have one single solution. Some couples abandon the attempt and either let sex die out completely or continue a lovemaking pattern marked by day-to-day sameness and repetition. This may mean making love once a week, in the same place, on the same day, and in the same way. It's all over in ten minutes, from start to finish. It isn't awful or unpleasant, just uninteresting and unexciting.

Some partners who are unhappy either with the demise of their sexual lives or with continuing sexual monotony look for sexual contacts outside of marriage. Some cultures have made mistresses or extramarital lovers practically an accepted solution to the problem of sexual boredom.

It doesn't have to be this way. Continued lovemaking

in a long-term relationship can be more satisfying and more interesting than that in any brief relationship. Sex therapist Dr. Ruth Westheimer states this beautifully in *Dr. Ruth's Guide to Good Sex:*

> There may be too much talk about sex in marriages or long relationships getting dull. I want to explain that it isn't the nature of the thing to be boring. Long sexual relationships offer pleasures you can't get any other way. Making love with the partner you have had for twenty years, who knows you better than anyone else, who has shared life's ups and downs with you, can be a royal pleasure.

If your sexual relationship has become dull, reestablishing intensity and excitement won't come automatically. It will require time and effort on your part. It's most likely to succeed if you and your partner have feelings of true affection for each other and a genuine interest in improving your sexual lives.

It's crucial to see yourselves as "lovers" again as well as "husband" and "wife." If your relationship has settled into dull marriage roles and you've stopped feeling like lovers, you may start to see both your partner and yourself as drab and unsexual. When you treat each other as household fixtures, sex can become blah. This can make an outside sex interest, which gives you or your partner the feeling of being exciting again, very inviting.

The concept of not *just* seeing yourself as husband and wife is very important. In our society, the role of being "husband" or "wife" has an entirely different emotional tone than that of "lover." The terms *husband* and *wife* imply reliability, solidness, security, duties, and responsibilities. *Lover* implies excitement, allure, passion, romance, play, fun, and, of course, love.

Now don't misunderstand me. You want, *you need to have,* those solid husband and wife qualities in a long-term relationship. But if you have *only* these qualities, your relationship may be solid but it may also be dull. In addition to security and responsibility, you need to regain the romance and excitement of being lovers again as well.

I'd like to suggest that you talk with your partner about how the two of you can get back that feeling of being lovers. Make it clear that he or she is special to you and valued and cherished. And don't make it clear only with words. Show your affection with caresses, hugs, and kisses, especially at times when it's not a prelude to lovemaking. Also tell your partner about the qualities you most appreciate in him or her. It's so easy, in a long-term relationship, to assume, "Oh, he [or she] already knows I appreciate that."

Get back that feeling of discovery and excitement in your relationship. Plan unusual vacations or projects; continuing to have adventures together is a way of keeping your lives interesting.

Reestablish some of those activities you remember from your courting days. Go out dancing, to a restaurant, or to movies or the theater together. Remember the flowers and little gifts that can give extra expressions of love. Don't save romance for special occasions like anniversaries or birthdays.

One important but infrequently thought of step is putting a muzzle on your television set. Keeping it on all evening, every evening can do more to make your lives dull and dampen your love life than almost anything else. Watching late-night TV especially can be terribly destructive to possible lovemaking opportunities. If there's a program coming on later that you feel you must watch, consider making love in the early evening. Then you can watch your program with a nice sexual glow. Or else, record the program on a VCR so you can watch it at your leisure.

Up to this point I have talked about what you can do to get back some of the *feelings* in your relationship. Making your *lovemaking* interesting and exciting again is another question.

## DISCUSS THIS
## CHAPTER WITH YOUR PARTNER

You and your partner really should review this chapter together. It will take commitment from each of you to recapture the feeling of being lovers again.

Making love at the same old time and in predictable ways may be monotonous, but it also brings a certain sense of security. This sense of security that comes from familiar routine causes inertia and resistance to change. Breaking out of this rut will be exciting and gratifying, but it will take effort and initiative from both of you.

## MAKE YOUR LOVEMAKING
## A HIGH PRIORITY

You must decide that being a lover to your partner is important in your life—more important, in fact, than most of your day-to-day activities. Lovemaking has to rank above doing the dishes, balancing the checkbook, or doing some extra paperwork you brought home from the office. Don't put off making love in order to start last-minute chores that don't have to be done right away. It's not something to save until you're tired at the end of a long day, when your body is telling you that it's time to go to sleep.

## HUG AND CARESS IN BED EVEN IF
## YOU'RE NOT PLANNING TO MAKE LOVE

Don't feel that bedtime caressing is only for the nights when you are planning to make love. Set aside some time before going to sleep, even if it's just a minute or two, for affection. It doesn't have to lead to sex. If you cuddle every night, you won't necessarily make love more frequently, but you'll certainly both feel more loved and loving.

## VARY WHEN AND WHERE
## YOU MAKE LOVE

Try making love at different times of the day. Go back to bed after breakfast, if you have the opportunity, or have a romantic lovemaking session in the middle of the afternoon with the sun streaming in your window.

Try making love in different places in your house as well. Consider the living room couch, or throw a sheet over some soft carpeting or a throw rug on the floor.

Plan an occasional night for a special romantic atmosphere. Use candles and music, perhaps a special wine, a fire in the fireplace—whatever your imagination comes up with. Planning together is fun, but don't overlook the delight that surprise can bring.

Let yourself be open to spontaneous lovemaking. If your partner suggests lovemaking at an unusual time, or when you aren't expecting it, or when you have other plans or other things on your mind, don't say no automatically. Break that negative habit. Let yourself feel young again— make love right on the spot. You may find it truly exhilarating.

## VARY LOVEMAKING
## TECHNIQUES AND POSITIONS

Discuss new petting and caressing techniques with your partner. Think how you can vary standard ways of caressing by starting on a different part of your partner's body, such as fingertips or toes. Try caressing each other with sensuous fabrics such as silk or satin, or use a feather brush, or try caressing with body oils.

Be adventurous. Try new lovemaking positions. If you usually make love with the woman lying on her back, try some variations. Let her bring her knees all the way up, wrap her legs around the man's waist, or bring them up over his shoulders. (She will feel a different kind of vaginal stimulation with her pelvis tilted like this).

Try making love with the woman kneeling on top, or lying on her stomach with a pillow under her pelvis, or kneeling at the edge of the bed while her partner enters her from behind. Let your imaginations run freely. Invent some positions of your own.

## GIVE YOUR PARTNER
## ALL THE WONDERFUL FEELINGS
## YOU CAN IMAGINE

Before lovemaking, try to imagine how you would like your partner to feel at the height of sexual excitement. Then concentrate on how you can give your partner all those delightful and wonderful feelings.

Think, too, of lovemaking as play. Give yourselves permission to be silly, curious, foolish, and joyful. Lovemaking isn't work, and it doesn't have to be serious.

## YOU WILL BOTH BE EXCITED ABOUT
## THE VARIETY IN YOUR LOVEMAKING

I realize that you can't keep discovering totally new ways of lovemaking every time, but that's not really the goal I'm suggesting. Rather, I'm trying to help you find ways to overcome a serious danger in all long-term sexual relationships: the danger of monotony.

If you use a variety of different caresses, different positions, different music, occasional lovemaking oils, and different places for sex, you will, of course, repeat yourself in time, but your love life certainly won't be boring. You'll be able to capture that sense of novelty and excitement that adds such spice to sex. If the two of you work together, discuss this chapter, and plan a new relationship together, you can change your own lives.

# Trying New Patterns of Lovemaking

A remarkable number of the older couples I see in my practice seem to be stuck on the idea that there's only one appropriate pattern for lovemaking—the one they've been following. Often this consists of a certain amount of foreplay leading to intercourse during which the man climaxes.

While some couples realistically expect that the woman will usually climax with clitoral stimulation, either before or after intercourse, a surprising number in this day and age still feel that the only valid way for the woman to climax is during intercourse. For them, lovemaking ends when the man climaxes or loses his erection. If she hasn't climaxed by then, they rarely make an attempt to have her do so by manual or oral stimulation. Often it's the woman herself who feels that climaxing outside of intercourse isn't natural or makes her uncomfortable. She'll say she wants to climax in the "natural" way.

What these couples consider "unnatural"—climaxing from manual or oral clitoral stimulation—is actually the natural way of climaxing for the majority of women. Female sexual response certainly seems to be designed for this method of stimulation. For an older couple to insist on mandatory climaxes during intercourse for both the man and the woman puts tremendous pressure on a man with a possibly already fragile erection reflex. If he doesn't get fully erect or doesn't maintain his erection, his partner remains frustrated —and he feels a failure.

One particular couple in their middle fifties related the wide variety of lovemaking patterns they had used on a single weekend. They had used these patterns not to be eccentric or outrageous, but simply to be comfortable and to adapt in a natural way to some of the changes of aging. I'll let Betty tell you about their experience:

> Bill and I were thinking about the different ways we made love last weekend. We hadn't planned any particular kind of sex at all. It was just the way it turned out.
>
> So many people we know feel that sex is a failure if it doesn't work out exactly the way it's supposed to—like if both of them don't climax. Bill and I feel that as we've gotten older we've outgrown that kind of foolishness. We've learned to enjoy our lovemaking for what it is—each time.
>
> For instance, this last Friday we came home late and tired. We got into bed with neither of us having any idea of making love. We started playing around a little, though, and we gradually got turned on. I caressed Bill's penis until he got hard, and we had intercourse for a little while, and then we tired out and quit. Neither of us climaxed, but we dropped off to sleep feeling happy and content.
>
> Saturday morning we could sleep late. We woke up cuddling and Bill started playing with me—first with his hand and then with his tongue. I just lay back in bed half asleep and enjoyed him licking me. It felt divine.
>
> My arthritis bothers me, though, first thing in the morning. I usually feel stiff when I first wake up, and I can't climax. So I asked Bill to come up in the bed where I could reach him, and I used my hand and mouth to get him hard. Then I rolled over onto my side and he slipped into my vagina from behind. That's the easiest way for me to get started when my arthritis is bothering me.
>
> We made love leisurely that way for a while. Then I rolled over onto my stomach and put a pillow under my hips, and

we just kept on with him on top of me. Finally, when my joints felt a little looser, I turned over on my back for some more. Eventually, Bill pulled out. He hadn't come, so I helped him to finish with my hand. It was fun, watching him come.

You know, we could've spoiled that delightful experience by finding fault with ourselves—because I hadn't climaxed, and because Bill didn't climax inside me. We didn't, though. We felt that our lovemaking was wonderful. We felt warm, close, and loving all day because of it.

Saturday night while we were in bed talking, Bill started playing with me again. I hadn't come either that morning or the night before, so this time I really was ready. He started licking my clitoris with his tongue while his fingers were in my vagina rubbing what I guess is my G-spot. That certainly feels terrific to me, and I climax most easily that way. I had a big climax which pleased Bill greatly (me, too!).

After resting a minute or two, I started to stroke him. He got partly hard, but he just didn't feel that he needed to come again or have more sex after having come that morning. He suggested we wait until the next day. He felt proud of the nice orgasm he had given me, and we both felt good.

Sunday morning we slept in again. We felt very snuggly and warm and petted each other until I got wet and he got hard, and this time he came inside me.

He offered to pet me to climax too, but I asked him to wait until after breakfast. (My arthritis is always better after I've moved around a bit.) He was glad to wait. We did go back to bed after eggs and bacon, and he had fun bringing me to another wonderful climax.

We don't always have so much lovemaking in a weekend, but this one was wonderful.

It wasn't that this couple had "so much" lovemaking but that they had so many little fragments of lovemaking.

They didn't have strict rules, so they accepted whatever aspect of lovemaking happened to come along, and they felt comfortable with it. In fact, *none* of their lovemaking episodes fit the rigid mythical model of sex: simple intercourse with the man always hard and ready to ejaculate and the woman climaxing during intercourse. But what was really important was that this older couple had truly learned how to appreciate sex and themselves. They were happy each time with whatever happened in their lovemaking, and they weren't critical of their own performance or their partner's. They have really learned what "making love" is all about.

# Bibliography

## Expanding Your Basic Sexual Knowledge

Brecher, Edward. *Love, Sex and Aging.* New York: Little, Brown & Co., 1984.

Budoff, Penny. *No More Menstrual Cramps and Other Good News.* New York: Penguin Books, 1980.

Butler, Robert, and Lewis, Myrna. *Sex After Sixty.* Boston: G.K. Hall, 1977.

Comfort, Alex. *A Good Age.* New York: Crown Publishers, 1976.

Cutler, Winnifred; Garcia, Celso-Ramon; and Edwards, David. *Menopause: A Guide for Women and the Men Who Love Them.* New York: Norton, 1983.

Goldenson, Robert, and Anderson, Kenneth. *The Language of Sex from A to Z.* New York: World Almanac, 1986.

Greenberger, Monroe, and Siegel, Mary Ellen. *What Every Man Should Know About His Prostate.* New York: Walker & Co., 1983.

Haeberle, Erwin. *The Sex Atlas.* New York: Seabury Press, 1978.

Hite, Shere. *The Hite Report.* New York: Dell Publishing Co., Inc., 1976.

———. *The Hite Report on Male Sexuality.* New York: Ballantine Books, 1981.

Masters, William; Johnson, Virginia; and Kolodny, Robert. *Masters and Johnson on Sex and Human Loving.* New York: Little, Brown & Co., 1982.

Starr, Bernard, and Weiner, Marcella. *The Starr Weiner Report on Sex and Sexuality in the Mature Years.* New York: McGraw-Hill, 1981.

Wolman, Benjamin, and Money, John. *Handbook of Human Sexuality.* Englewood Cliffs, NJ: Prentice-Hall, 1980.

Zilbergelt, Bernie. *Male Sexuality.* New York: Bantam Books, 1978.

## Professional Books and Textbooks

Kaplan, Helen Singer. *Disorders of Sexual Desire.* New York: Brunner/Mazel, 1979.

———. *The Evaluation of Sexual Disorders.* New York: Brunner/Mazel, 1983.

———. *The New Sex Therapy.* New York: Brunner/Mazel, 1974.

Kolodny, Robert; Masters, William; and Johnson, Virginia. *Textbook of Sexual Medicine.* New York: Little, Brown & Co., 1979.

Masters, William, and Johnson, Virginia. *Human Sexual Inadequacy.* New York: Bantam Books, 1970.

Meyer, John K., Schmidt, Chester, and Wise, Thomas. *Clinical Management of Sexual Disorders,* 2nd ed. Baltimore: Williams & Wilkins, 1983.

## Expanding Your Knowledge of Sexual Technique

Barbach, Lonnie. *For Each Other: Sharing Sexual Intimacy.* Garden City, NY: Anchor Books, 1983.

———. *For Yourself: The Fulfillment of Female Sexuality.* Anchor Books, 1976.

Brauer, Alan P., and Brauer, Donna. *ESO: How You and Your Lover Can Give Each Other Hours of Extended Sexual Orgasm.* New York: Warner Books, 1983.

Comfort, Alex. *The Joy of Sex.* New York: Crown Publishers, 1972.

———. *More Joy of Sex.* New York: Crown Publishers, 1973.

Heiman, Julia; LoPiccolo, Leslie; and Lo Piccolo, Joseph. *Becoming Orgasmic: A Sexual Growth Program for Women.* New York: Prentice-Hall, 1976.

Ladas, Alice; Wipply, Beverly; and Perry, John. *The "G" Spot.* New York: Holt, Reinhart & Winston, 1982.

Nowinski, Joseph. *Becoming Satisfied: A Man's Guide to Sexual Fulfillment.* New York: Prentice-Hall, 1980.

Penney, Alexandra. *How to Make Love to a Man.* New York: Clarkson and Potter, Inc., 1981.

Westheimer, Ruth. *Dr. Ruth's Guide for Married Lovers.* New York: Warner Books, 1986.

———. *Dr. Ruth's Guide to Good Sex.* New York: Warner Books, 1983.

## Erotica

Barbach, Lonnie. *Erotic Interludes: Tales Told by Women.* New York: Doubleday, 1986.

———. *Pleasures: Women Write Erotica.* New York: Harper & Row, 1984.

Friday, Nancy. *Forbidden Flowers.* New York: Pocket Books, 1975.

———. *My Secret Garden.* New York: Pocket Books, 1973.

Kronhausen, Phyllis, and Kronhausen, Eberhard. *The Complete Book of Erotic Art.* East Brunswick, NJ: Bell Publishing, 1978.

Nin, Anais. *Delta of Venus.* New York: Bantam Books, 1969.

# Index

ACE inhibitors, 163, 166–167, 170

Adrenal glands, 15

Afternoon lovemaking, 62

Alcohol consumption, 20–21, 160, 176–182, 222, 227
long-term effects, 176–179
single dose effects, 179–180

Alpha blockers, 163

Amphetamines, 185, 186–187

Androgens, 15

Anginal pain, 160

Angiotensin converting enzyme inhibitors. *See* ACE inhibitors

Antianxiety medications, 174

Antibodies against sperm and testicles, 178

Antidepressants, 172–173

Antihistamines, 173

Antihypertensive medications, 162–169, 170, 222

Anxiety, 4, 16, 45–46, 48–49, 53, 76, 84–85, 212–217, 226

Appetizer, sexual, 120–122

Arrhythmia medications, 160, 163

Arteriosclerosis, 11, 12, 222, 227, 232
estrogen and, 29–30, 35, 39

Arthritis, 137–147
intercourse positions, 142–145
manual stimulation and, 146
oral lovemaking and, 145, 146

Atrophic vaginitis, 27, 150, 151

Attitudes, 100. *See also* Inhibitions
arthritis and, 139, 146–147

Back pain, 137–147

Bathing/showering, 63–64, 92, 103

Benign prostatic hypertrophy (BPH), 189–191, 194–195
Beta blockers, 160, 164–165, 168
Blood pressure
    high (*see* Hypertension)
    penile, 224
BPH (benign prostatic hypertrophy), 189–191
Breakfast, romantic, 64–65
Breast cancer, 34, 37
Breasts, caressing, 28, 70–72, 82–83
Bubble baths, 63–64
Budoff, Penny Wise, 39
Bulbocaversal reflex, 224

Calcium, 15, 19, 42
Calcium channel blockers, 163, 166, 167, 170
Cancer
    breast, 34, 37
    endometrial, 32
    prostatic, 190, 193–194, 196–198
    uterine, 32, 35
Caresses. *See* Touching, sexual
Changes of aging
    adaptation to, 5
    advantages of, 14
    awareness of, 9
    in males, 3–14, 48–49 (*see also* Men, older)
    reasons for, 10–12
Cholesterol, high density lipoprotein, 20–21
Cigarette smoking, 21, 29, 183–185, 222, 227
Cleanliness, 91, 92, 103–104
Climax. *See* Orgasm

Clitoris, stimulation of, 28–29, 100–101, 102, 105, 109
Cocaine, 185, 186
Communication of feelings, 56, 140, 147
Cunnilingus, 102–106, 114
    G-spot stimulation and, 109, 111–112
    techniques, 104–105

Depression, 145–146
    after heart attacks, 160–161
    hypothyroidism and, 223
    after hysterectomy, 202–203
Diabetes, 20, 184, 222–223, 227
Dildos, 40
Direct physical stimulation.
    *See also* Manual stimulation; Oral stimulation
    of clitoris, 28–29, 100–101, 102, 105, 109
    need for, 5–6, 46, 47
    of penis, 5–6, 13, 46–47, 75, 77, 80–83, 86, 92–95, 215
Dispareunia, 148–153
Distractions, 51–60
Diuretics, 163, 164, 170
Dreams, sexual, 25
Drugs. *See* Medications; "Recreational" drugs
Dyspareunia deep/thrusting, 150, 151–152
    superficial, 149–151
    treatment, 152–153

Ejaculations
    changes with aging, 7–8, 13, 48–49

refractory period following, 9–10
retrograde, 195–196
Endometrial biopsy, 38
Endometrial cancer, 32
Endometriosis, 38, 151–153
Endometrium, and hormone replacement therapy, 33–34
Endorphins, 139
Erection(s). *See also* Impotence; Penis
anxiety and, 76, 77, 212–217
changes with aging, 11–12
complexity of, 11
concerns about, 45–48
fading of, 3–4, 7, 10, 48, 85, 213
firmness of, 6–7, 12, 47–48
nighttime or morning, 220–221
physical stimulation and, 6
problem evaluation, 211–217, 219–228
spontaneous, loss of, 3–4, 5, 6, 46–47, 75, 89–90, 215
Teasing Technique and, 85–88
testosterone and, 16, 18, 21
time between, 9–10
Erection mechanism, 232
tests of, 220–221
Erection-aid devices, 225–226, 227, 228–229
Estrogen, 16
acute withdrawal symptoms, 26
chronic deprivation of, 29–30
forms prescribed, 37
levels, 25, 26–28

prostate cancer and, 197
testosterone replacement and, 19
Estrogen creams, 32, 150
Estrogen replacement therapy (ERT), 31–42
atrophic vaginitis and, 150
contraindications, 37–38
effects, 31–32
after hysterectomy, 207
pregnancy and, 39–40
progesterone added to, 33–34, 36, 37
uterine contractions and, 28
Estrogen/progesterone cycling, 33–34, 36, 37
Exercises/exercising
arthritis and, 141
and blood pressure, 167
heart condition and, 157–158
Kegel, 41, 125–129
Expectations, erroneous, 45–49

Fantasies, sexual, 5–6, 22, 56–57, 132
Feathering, 65–66, 71, 249
Fellatio, 83, 90–96
climax during, 95
inhibitions about, 90
techniques, 92–96
women's enjoyment of, 91–92, 93
Flowers, 62
Fluoride, 42
Focusing thoughts, 55–56, 84–85, 225

Goals, long-range, 55
Goldstein, Irwin, 183

G-spot, 107–111
  location, 107
  stimulation of, 108–110

Heart attacks, 37
  energy expenditure after,
    155–156
  estrogen and, 30, 35, 39
  sexual relations following,
    154–161
  testosterone and, 20
  of women, 159
Heart problems
  sexual activity and, 154–
    161
  testosterone and, 19
Heroin, 187
Herpes, 151
High-blood-pressure
    medications, 162–169,
    170, 222
Hot flashes, 26, 31, 39
Hypertension, 38, 162–169,
    222
  medications, 162–169
Hypothyroidism, 223, 227
Hysterectomy, 199–207
  abdominal, 200
  complete, 200
  effects of, 202–203
  estrogen replacement
    therapy and, 207
  myths about, 201–202
  reasons for performing, 201
  sexual desire and, 205–207
  sexual relations following,
    204–205, 206–207
  testosterone administration
    after, 206
  vaginal, 200

Impotence, 12. *See also*
    Erection(s)
  alcohol abuse and, 177–180
  cigarette smoking, excessive,
    and, 183–184
  cocaine use and, 186
  evaluation and treatment,
    218–230
  marijuana use and, 186
  opiates and, 187
  perineal prostatectomy and,
    197
  testosterone replacement
    and, 16
Inhibitions
  arthritis and, 146–147
  to oral lovemaking, 90–92,
    97–98, 103
  overcoming, 51, 57–60
Insecurity thoughts, 52
  controlling, 55–57
Intercourse. *See also*
    Lovemaking
  without climaxing, 118–120,
    121, 122, 123–124
  frequency of, 7
  painful, 150–153
  positions after heart attack,
    142–143
  positions for limited
    mobility, 142–145
  prolongation of, 8–9,
    118–120
IPV, 225

Johnson, Virginia, 7, 40, 100,
    181, 185

Kegel, Arnold, 126
Kegel exercises, 41, 125–129

Kidneys, 19, 222, 223
Kinsey, A., 100

Liver, 15, 18, 19, 20, 37, 222
   alcohol and, 178, 179
Long-term relationships,
   245–254
Lovemaking, 121–122. *See also*
   Intercourse
   brief, 117, 120–122
   half-asleep, 122–124
   as high priority, 248
   improvement after forty,
      12–14
   mutuality in, 14
   as play, 250
   prolonged, 12–14, 117–120
   spontaneous, 47
   starting, 81
   variety in, 59–60, 61–73
   with warm oil, 66–68
Lower back pain, 137–147
Lubricants, sexual, 41–42,
      66–68, 71, 72, 80–83, 103,
      118, 121, 122, 133
   arthritis and, 141–142
   flavored, 72, 92
   following hysterectomy, 205
   warmed, 66–68, 83

Male sexuality, erroneous
   expectations about, 45–50
Males. *See* Men, older
Mammography, 38
Manual stimulation, 10, 50,
      79, 159, 251
   arthritis and, 146
   of clitoris, 101
MAO inhibitors, 173
Marijuana, 185–186

Marriage roles, 246–247
Massage, 81, 141
   with warm oil, 66–68
Masters, William, 7, 40, 100,
      181, 185
Masturbation, 25, 130–133
   as test of erection
      mechanism, 216, 220
   vaginal insertions during,
      40–41
   varying techniques, 133
Medications
   antianxiety, 174
   antidepressant, 172–173
   antihistamines, 173
   for benign prostatic
      hypertrophy, 195
   for erection problems, 225,
      228
   for heart problems, 160
   for hypertension, 162–170,
      222
   prescription, 171–175
   schedule, 140–141
   sexual side-effects, 160–169,
      171–175, 217, 226–227
Men, older
   changes of aging, 3–14
   partner's understanding of,
      74–79
   prolonged lovemaking and,
      117–118
Menopause, 25–30. *See also*
   Estrogen replacement
   therapy
   sexual pleasure after, 23–24,
      28
   surgical, 200, 207
Mental obstacles, overcoming,
   51–60

Mental stimulation, 5–6
Methyltestosterone, 18, 20
METS, 155–156
Mirrors, 69–70
Monoamine oxidase (MAO)
    inhibitors, 173
Morning erections, 214
Morning lovemaking, 72–73,
    123–124, 249
Mouth, 92, 93, 106. *See also*
    Oral lovemaking
Muscles, sexual, exercises to
    strengthen, 126–129
Music, 62

Narcotics, 187
Nighttime erections, 214,
    220–221
Nipples, stimulating, 70–72,
    83–84
Nitroglycerine, 160
Nocturnal penile tumescence
    (NPT) test, 220–221

Oil, lubricating. *See*
    Lubricants, sexual
Older men and women. *See*
    Men, older; Women,
    older
Oophorectomy, 200, 206
Opiates, 187
Oral lovemaking, 10, 50, 79,
    89–98, 159, 251. *See also*
    Cunnilingus; Fellatio
    arthritis and, 145, 146
    inhibitions about, 97–98,
    103
    woman's guide to, 89–98
Orgasms, 7, 53

difficulty in having, 4, 7–8,
    48–49
multiple, 110–111
simultaneous, 116
of women, 99–100, 115–116
Osteoporosis, 29, 32, 35–36,
    42
Ovarian cysts, 151, 200
Ovaries, 181, 200

Pain, lower back, 137–147
Painful intercourse, 150–153
Pelvic congestion syndrome,
    152
Pelvic infections, 151–152
Penile implants, 198, 219, 230,
    231–242
    advantages and
    disadvantages, 235–240
    candidates for, 240–241
    flexible, 236, 239
    inflatable, 232–234, 235, 237
    self-contained inflatable
    rod, 235, 239–240
    semirigid rod, 234, 236,
    238–239
Penile injections, 227, 229
Penile vascular surgery,
    229–230
Penis, 82. *See also* Erection(s);
    Impotence
    blood pressure in, 224
    blood supply to, 11
    lubricating, 82–83, 123
    physical stimulation of, 5–6,
    13, 46–47, 75, 77, 80–83,
    86, 92–95, 215
    sensitivity, 82
Peyronies disease, 224

Phenoxybenzamine, 195
Phenylpropanolamine, 196
Physical stimulation. *See*
    Direct physical
    stimulation
Pituitary gland, 20, 178, 223
Polycythemia, 19
Positions in lovemaking
    arthritis and, 142–145
    following heart attack,
        158–159
    varying, 59, 249–250
Pregnancy, 39–40
Priapism, 20
Priorities, 53–55, 58
Progesterone, 33–34, 153
Prolactin elevation, 223–224
Prolongation of lovemaking,
    12–14, 117–120
Prostate cancer, 190, 193–194,
    196–198
Prostate gland, 188–189, 224
    enlargement of, 189–191,
        194
    testosterone replacement
        and, 19–20
Prostatectomies, 194, 197
Prostatic congestion, 192–193
Prostatitis, 191–193
    Kegel exercises and, 129
Prostatodynia, 192–193
Prostatosis, 192–193
Provera, 37
Pulse rate, 156
    beta blockers and, 160

"Recreational" drugs, 185–187
Rectal examinations, 198
Refractory period, 9–10

Resentments, 54, 55
Retrograde ejaculation,
    195–196
Romance, 61, 62, 118,
    246–247, 249

Scott, Brantley, 242
Semen, 95
Sensate focus exercises, 225
Sexual activity, benefits of,
    139, 161
Sexual desire
    hysterectomy and, 205–206
    Kegel exercises and, 126
    menopause and, 28
    myths about, 49–50
    testosterone and, 15–16, 21,
        25
Sexual tension, building, 118,
    119–120, 121, 124
Sexual Therapy Clinic of San
    Antonio, 6, 212, 218, 219
    impotence evaluation and
    treatment program,
        218–230
Sexually transmitted
    infections, 150–151
Sjogrens Syndrome, 141–142
Sleep, erections during, 214,
    220–221
Smoking. *See* Cigarette
    smoking
Snap-gauge test, 221
"Speed." *See* Amphetamines
Sperm, 20, 177, 178
Spontaneity, 249
Stamp test, 221
Stimulation. *See* Direct
    physical stimulation

Stress. *See* Anxiety
Surgery
  for benign prostatic
    hypertrophy, 194
  penile implant, 231–242
  for prostate cancer, 196–197
  on vascular system of penis,
    229–230
Sympathetic nervous system
  blockers, 163, 164–166,
  170

Teasing Technique, 85–88
Testicles
  alcohol consumption and,
    177, 178, 179
  examination of, 224
Testosterone, 11, 15–21. *See
  also* Testosterone
  replacement
  alcohol consumption and,
    177–178, 179
  hypothyroidism and, 223
  following hysterectomy, 206
  level of, 11, 12, 16–17, 20,
    21, 24–25, 87
  prostate cancer and, 197
  sexual desire and, 15–16,
    25, 28
Testosterone replacement,
  16–21, 228
Thiazide diuretics, 163, 164,
  167
Thrombophlebitis, 37
Thyroid gland, 223
Time of lovemaking, 58–60,
  62
Time priorities, 53–55, 58, 248
Touching, sexual, 28, 58–60,
  70–72, 82, 248, 249

Tranquilizers, 174–175
Transurethral resection (TUR),
  194
Treadmill test, 157, 159
Tricyclic antidepressants, 172

Ulcer medications, 174
Urinary symptoms
  menopause and, 27
  prostatic enlargement and,
    189–190
  vaginitis and, 151
Urological examination,
  224–225
Uterine cancer, 32, 35
Uterine myomas, 151
Uterine prolapse, 201
Uterus, 199–200
  cervix, 200
  defined, 199–200

Vagina
  estrogen deficiency and, 27,
    37, 39
  G-spot, 107–111
  lubricating, 67–68, 69, 72,
    80–81, 103, 108, 113, 118,
    122, 123, 141–142, 150,
    205
  maintaining tone of, 40–41,
    125–128
  vibrator stimulation of,
    113–114
Vaginal dryness, 27, 39,
  41–42, 150
Vaginismus, 149, 152
Vaginitis, 150–152
Variations, sexual, 61–73,
  249–254
Vasodilators, 163, 166, 170

Venereal warts, 151
Vibrators, 40–41, 111–115, 133
    stimulation techniques,
        113–114
Vitamin D, 42

Walsh, Patrick, 197
Westheimer, Ruth, 94–95, 97,
    246
Women, 13, 25, 76–77
    climaxes, 99–100, 110–111,
        115–116

Women, older
    alcohol and, 181
    enhancing pleasure of,
        99–115
    hormone levels, 24–25
    sexual desire of, 22–29
Worries, 52–57, 157

Yeast infections, 150

Zinc, 190–191, 192

# For More Information . . .

Dr. Rosenthal is the medical director of The Sexual Therapy Clinic of San Antonio. To contact the clinic, please call 512-697-8351.

If you have found this book valuable and would like continuing, up-to-date information, Dr. Rosenthal suggests you consider subscribing to the newsletter *Sex Over Forty*. Founded by Dr. Rosenthal in 1982, the newsletter gives older men and women the important information they need to have full and satisfying sex lives. A one-year subscription to *Sex Over Forty* is available for $36.00 from Newsletter, c/o Saul H. Rosenthal, M.D., 7711 Louis Pasteur, Ste. 812, San Antonio, TX 78229.